Waking Up Sober in a Convent

Waking Up Sober in a Convent

And Other Spiritual Adventures

Kathy Stolecki

ISBN: 978-1-4839-08731
ISBN: 1-4839-08739

Library of Congress Control Number: 2012913494

Any people depicted in stock imagery provided by Thinkstock are models, and such images are being used for illustrative purposes only.
Certain stock imagery © Thinkstock.

This book is printed on acid-free paper.

Because of the dynamic nature of the Internet, any web addresses or links contained in this book may have changed since publication and may no longer be valid. The views expressed in this work are solely those of the author and do not necessarily reflect the views of the publisher, and the publisher hereby disclaims any responsibility for them.

This book is dedicated to my Parents, with a special dedication to my Dad, Grandpa and Grandma:

You are my 'Three Musketeers' on the Other Side.

Acknowledgements

So many people have loved and supported me on my journey and during the writing of this book.

To my Family, especially my Mom and Dad, my Grandparents,
my Sisters and Brothers, my Aunts and Uncles:
Thanks for your love and support.

To the Sisters in the Convent, my Friends, near and far;
also my Sponsors; my Spiritual Directors, Sister Pam, Father John;
my therapists, especially Sister Carole and Joan;
my pastors, Rev. Brad, Rev. Millie and Rev. Suzette,
who have all nurtured my spiritual growth.

Thanks to my Singing Partner, Sue, for making the
Serenity Sisters possible.
I value your friendship and have enjoyed our time together.

Thanks to my friend Judy for giving me the idea for the book's title.

Special thanks to my Sweetheart, for your love and support,
for encouraging me to make writing a priority; for helping me edit
my work and giving invaluable input on the flow of this book.
I love you dearly. Thank you for adding spice to my life
and for your support throughout this process.

Thanks my loving pets, especially Jessi and Julio, for their
unconditional love. They have taught me so much about the
meaning of love.

And Last but not Least: to my Higher Power, my Creator, whose
loving Presence has always been with me.
Thanks for Sobriety, for Serenity, for the Music and for
Showing Me the Way to Truth, to You.

Table of Contents

Introduction

I remember sitting in church on Sunday morning, before the Mass began. I was about five years old. The church was silent. I sat quietly and looked around at the stained glass windows and the various statues: Jesus on the Cross, the Blessed Mother, St. Joseph and a few other Saints. Up high on the wall behind the altar was a circular stained glass window with a picture of the Blessed Mother holding the baby Jesus. A warm feeling glowed in my heart. I felt like **ET** with my *heart light* all aglow, recognizing the Mother Ship.

Fast forward . . . now I'm 21 years old . . . . walking through the halls of a Convent I entered eighteen months earlier, only now I'm six months sober, slowly waking up. Then one day it suddenly hits me, "OMG! I'm in a Convent! I'll be taking vows in a few months—I'm going to be a NUN!! This is happening way too fast!! I gotta slow this down. What do I do now???"

How did I get here? And where was I going?

This is my God story, my personal journey with God. During my 40+ years on the planet there have been times when I've felt God's loving, peaceful presence and times when I've felt utterly alone. I faced my alcoholism and have overcome addiction. I experienced struggle and growth while in the Convent. I finally Came Out and reached a deep level of self acceptance, reconciling my sexuality with God. I experienced the pain of rejection, the death of loved ones, the sadness of loneliness, but I also experienced an enormous amount of joy along the way. My concept of God has changed over the years due to the experiences I'll be sharing with you. The changes, though positive, have come with a price. It was often scary and painful. At times I didn't know if I would survive, or if I even wanted to.

I now know that God, the Angels, my Spirit Guides and Loved Ones on the other side have been with me through it all and are always with me, even when I'm not aware of their presence. I have moved from *believing* to KNOWING that life is eternal and there is a loving God.

Truly—All is Well.

My story is no more special than yours. I hope that by sharing my God story, you will become more aware of your own, and that you will see the loving Hand of God working in your life.

Peace, Love, Hugs,
Kathy

PS:
Names have been changed to protect others' privacy.

During this journey, I have composed songs that reflect my soul's yearnings and my heart's desires. You will find the words to some of my songs throughout the book as well as in the final section, 'The Story Behind the Music'. The music is available on my web site: www.KathyStolecki.com or www.WakingUpSober.com

PPS: Originally published under my pen name, Katharine Rose Marie, I decided I needed to 'Come Out' again and claim my story. My original reasons for using a pen name fell away over the past several months and it became clear to me that using a pen name was another form of hiding-out, another form of shame. With several nudges from my friend Jodi and confirmation from Spirit via my Spiritualist community and encouragement from my family and friends, I decided to let go of another layer of shame (Yes!) and put my name on my story. Katharine Rose Marie does have special meaning to me: Katharine is my first name, Marie is my confirmation name and Katharine Rose was my convent name. However, standing in Peace and Light won out in the end. ☺

Chapter 1

Early Influences—
How It All Began

I grew up in a large Catholic family, the second of eight. I was always excited when my parents told us we were having another baby. Babies always brought joy to our home. I loved the way Mom would coo and talk to the baby, her face lit up with joy.

There's something special about growing up in a large family. My sisters and brothers were my best friends. We had our share of fights, of course, but it taught us how to get along. My parents did something right in how they raised us because we all love each other deeply and remain close to this day.

My parents were devout Catholics. At one time both Mom and Dad had considered a religious vocation. Then Mom decided she wanted children and Dad, well, he never really told us why he changed his mind. It could have been his experiences in the Army. When he decided to have a family, he wanted lots of kids. As an only child, Dad was rather lonely. He wanted a large family to ensure his kids wouldn't go through what he'd experienced.

I went to Catholic grade school through the 8th grade. In second grade I saw a movie about Jesus. It showed Him being tortured, carrying the cross and being crucified. I cried as He carried the cross through the streets, people mocking Him. At that moment I

1

fell in love with Jesus. Dad would often say, "The greatest ambition in life is to strive to become a Saint." I must have been pretty young when I thought "then that's what I want to be." In religion class I wrote how when I grew up I would sing songs about God to let people know how much God loves them.

Dad always hoped that at least one of his kids would have a religious vocation. A religious vocation is when a person feels called to enter religious life, either to be a priest, a sister or a brother. When we said grace at supper time, Dad added an extra Our Father, Hail Mary and Glory Be for vocations. No pressure, right? We got the message. But none of us took it seriously. I mean, what does a call to religious life look like, anyway?

Dad was a strong family man. He knew the importance of family vacations. I'm sure he needed some down time with juggling work and raising a family. With such a large brood Dad needed to be crafty to ensure that family vacations happened yearly and were affordable. He bought a used camper that had been damaged in an accident. He fixed it up and off we went on weekend adventures. Sometimes we took off for a week or two, camping in such places as Long Island, Connecticut, Jersey Shore. We even went to Florida every three years to enjoy Disney World and visit Dad's childhood friend Uncle Sal and his family.

They say camping is a bonding experience. It sure brought us closer together as a family. I have many wonderful memories: fighting through the waves off Long Island, riding bikes or hiking on various trails (baby stroller en tow), watching the blue and yellow flames of the evening campfire as we roasted marshmallows. Then there were those tense moments. For instance, Dad always drove. Mom was the navigator—the map reader. She hated it. Dad would ask her a question, such as, how much further before we should look for our next route. Mom would get flustered. She might have been good at it if she hadn't felt so pressured. Frustrated, Dad would grab the map and try to drive and read the map at the same time. Talk about scary! The tension was so thick that you could cut it with a knife. We would sit quietly in the back seat, holding our breath, hoping the moment would pass quickly and safely. We did get lost a few times, and thereafter, Dad would occasionally toot the horn and exclaim, "We're on the right road, kids!" Dad knew how to turn any situation around with his charming sense of humor.

Once we reached the campground we had to set up camp. That meant putting up the awning, creating our dining area. It was a tedious process. The four oldest kids were assigned a pole to hold onto as Dad attached the awning to it. Then we were supposed to raise the poles all at once to create the roof. Occasionally one of our poles got jammed and it slowed everyone else down. Dad would run from pole to pole, getting it all situated. As I'm describing it now, it doesn't sound that bad. Guess you had to be there.

As you can imagine, we outgrew the camper pretty quickly. Mom and Dad slept in the camper with the younger ones. Dad purchased a used tent for us girls. It was cool having our own space. Sometimes we forgot how to put it up. Each pole had a piece of masking tape with black magic marker indicating which poles went together—A with A, B with B. It was a good system, until the letters faded and we didn't know which pole went with which. We got frustrated trying to figure it out, but eventually we managed and made up our bedroom, complete with pillows and sleeping bags. For the most part, we had a great time camping.

I still remember camping at Hither Hills camp ground at Montauk Point on Long Island. We made friends with a couple of kids, Jen, Lori and Justin. We had a blast. They taught us how to fake fight. One night I threw a couple of fake punches at Justin, and a man grabbed me and said, "Jesus Christ, I thought you guys were fighting!" We really fooled him! We went back to camp to share this with Mom and Dad. "Did you tell the guy not to use the Lord's name in vain?" Dad replied. Yeah, Dad took things like cursing quite seriously. But he had his playful side. He could be heard saying things like "Live it up, kids. We're on vacation." He made the best sand castles and taught us how to fight through the ocean waves and then body surf back to shore.

3

For many years Dad played Santa Claus, aka, St. Nicholas, for us kids and the kids in the neighborhood. Dad was so creative. He told stories about the elves, how they made the toys and about the reindeer waiting for him on our roof. One year St. Nicholas gave my sister Sue a watch for her future career as a nurse. She could use the second hand to take her patient's pulse. As he gave the gift to Sue he spoke of how important it was to be of service to others. Service to God and humanity was very important to Dad.

Some weekends Dad put us to work on a project. We gathered wood for the wood-burning stoves so we could heat the house in the winter time. We dug a ditch to install a dry well for the laundry room. One of our major projects was when we installed an above ground swimming pool that our friends gave us. We dug a large hole to make the pool deeper. There were a few huge boulders we had to roll out using steel rods. When the time came to put up the pool, Dad enlisted the help of his friends at the local volunteer fire department. They brought over their tanker to help fill the pool. It was all quite an experience. When there weren't any major projects on the list, Dad had us clean out the garage or wash the car or camper. Although we complained to each other about the chores, it instilled in us a sense of family and a strong work ethic.

While Dad was the strong presence in our family, Mom was more quiet and nurturing. She was a stay-at-home Mom, raising the kids, making the meals, and doing the laundry, which never seemed to end. "Where's Mom?" someone would ask. "In the laundry room" was the usual reply. Dad called her 'St. June of the Laundry Room'. Mom had her novena cards to the Blessed Mother and other Saints lined up on the window sill, prayerfully going about her work. She taught us how to dust, vacuum, clean the bathroom and do dishes. Mom also modeled a childlike faith in God and the Blessed Mother. I often came home from school to find Mom snoozing on the couch with her Rosary beads in hand. Mom made each of our birthdays special by allowing us to request what we wanted for our birthday dinner.

In the summer we opened our pool and grew a vegetable garden. Mom tended the garden, then she'd jump in the pool to cool off and play with us. She organized diving contests for us and our neighborhood friends. We took the different floatation toys and piled them high on the deck, making an obstacle to dive over. One summer Mom helped me make a sling shot as we sat on the back porch steps. She had been a tomboy growing up and seemed happy that I was a tomboy too.

If you're not familiar with Catholicism, let me fill you in. There are a lot of rules! If you follow the teachings closely, like my parents did, you quickly become aware of what you should and shouldn't do. For instance, we observed Lent by saying the Rosary as a family every weekday before supper. We didn't eat meat on Fridays during Lent. We attended church every Sunday and on Holy Days of Obligation. We went to confession monthly during school time, since we attended Catholic school. The Catholic teachings focused on following the rules in order to get to Heaven.

'Don't question authority' is the message I got. Dad was very clear on what constituted God's will: "If it didn't come from the Pope's mouth, then God didn't say it." This was a very rigid approach to life. This approach also encouraged not thinking for oneself, and so I became a follower. I hated getting into trouble and would do all I could to make others happy. I also got the idea that our bodies were bad and sex should be saved only for marriage and for making babies.

I was a shy child. Despite my loving family, I didn't feel very lovable. I was a chubby kid, but I felt obese. I felt ugly and empty inside. I felt like an outsider at school—like I was on the outside looking in. I felt different and did my best to please others in order to fit in.

I was a closet tomboy at school, only showing my tomboy colors at home. One day at school during recess the boys were playing soccer. I was standing by my classmate, Marie, as we watched them play. I got so into the game that as I watched a boy kick the soccer ball, I kicked too, kicking poor Marie in the leg! I was as shocked as she! Embarrassed and apologetic, I tried to explain that I'd gotten too caught up in the game. She moved away from me, rubbing her leg. In my mind I associated enjoying sports and being a tomboy with having crushes on girls. I was afraid that if others knew I was a tomboy they'd discover my secret. I told myself this was just a stage I was going through. I'd outgrow it. At least I hoped so.

In 8th Grade a Sister came to talk to my class about religious vocations. She played the Paul McCartney song 'Someone's Knocking at the Door' and spoke of 'The Call'. I was secretly curious, but never let anyone know about it. I had always felt different. Maybe this was where I belonged?

My freshman year of high school was scary at first. I went from a small Catholic grade school, graduating from 8th grade with a class of 8 students, to a high school where the graduating class ran close to 70 students. It was pretty intimidating. My sister Sue was two grades ahead of me. She introduced me to a nice group of girls and we all became friends.

At the tender age of fourteen I discovered how alcohol could sooth my painful insecurity. I had actually been exposed to alcohol for many years prior, as we occasionally asked our parents for a sip (a 'zip', to be exact) of their rum n coke. I loved the warm feeling the alcohol gave me. As we got older we got to make their drinks. We took extra zips, refilled with coke, then took it out to them, be granted another zip as a reward for making their drink for them, and were thus introduced to alcohol. Occasionally on Sunday after church Dad would allow us to have a small glass of beer. I hated the taste of beer back then and opted for soda instead. Mom and Dad saw their own fathers' struggle with alcohol and didn't want it to be a problem for us. They introduced it to us early to take the mystery out of it. They meant well, but unfortunately it just didn't work that way.

So at the age of fourteen, after getting drunk on 2 beers on Halloween night, I was off and running. I should have seen the writing on the wall that night. My best buddy Tommy was out with his friends checking out the trick or treating scene. When our paths crossed he playfully grabbed my can of shaving cream and took off running. I chased him down and swung my bag of candy over his head, trying to get my shaving cream back. He stopped running, leaned over in pain, grabbing his head. I forgot I had my flashlight in the bag! His head was bleeding. The Sheriff was out on patrol, saw us and stopped his car. "Is everything alright over there?" he yelled. I whispered to Tommy, "I'm so sorry! I forgot my flashlight's in there. Please, walk away . . . walk away . . ." and he did. He went home and his Mom looked over his wound. He was going to be ok. She was cool and didn't make a big deal out of it. I felt horrible and told myself "never again". My resolve lasted until the next drinking opportunity came along.

I made the varsity basketball team as a freshman and that boosted my confidence a bit. I dated a boy two years older than me. He really liked me. I wasn't sure how I felt. It felt nice to be liked, but how did I feel about *him*? I was confused. We dated through freshman year and he took me to the prom. Then when he wanted more from me sexually, I got scared and broke up with him. I made honor roll and played varsity softball, even started as a freshman—another confidence boost. But I grew distant from my friends due to the time it took for practice and games. I experienced some success with softball and, according to one friend, got 'cocky'. When I looked around I realized my circle of friends had gradually disappeared.

10th grade was a tough year for me. I was sad, lonely and depressed. I hung out with my fellow 'out-casts' and was too embarrassed to share my feelings with anyone, even with my sisters. I didn't want them to think me a loser. I drank whenever the opportunity presented itself, even sneaking a small bottle of Jack Daniels into my locker at school. Part of me wanted to get caught because I knew I needed help of some sort. The other part of me was afraid of being caught and getting into trouble. I actually never did drink it at school, and I never got caught with it.

Then one day I found a copy of Norman Vincent Peale's book 'The Power of Positive Thinking' on our kitchen counter. I still don't know how it got there, but that book saved my life. It introduced me to the idea that our thoughts are powerful and that I could use different Bible verses to change my outlook on life. My favorites were: I can do all things through Christ who strengthens me. All Things are Possible with God. Wow! Seeing the Bible this way was totally new to me. I started to apply these ideas and felt more confident and at ease. I claimed my faith as my own rather than just 'inheriting' my parents' religion.

I still drank every chance I got, which wasn't really that often. But when I did, it was with the intention of getting a 'buzz'. I was too serious, always worried whether others liked me and if I was acceptable. Under the warm glow of alcohol I felt free! I was less self-conscious and more comfortable in my own skin. In NY at that time the legal age to buy alcohol was 18. My sisters and I knew a few people who could buy it for us but most of the time we'd just sneak some from our parent's liquor cabinet. It didn't take much to get a nice buzz.

At one point I made a deal with God: "I won't drink for three months, and You take away the arthritis in Grandpa's hip." Grandpa, or 'Pop' as the adults called him, had fallen on the dance floor at the German Alps Festival in upstate New York one summer while dancing with Mom. He was fooling around, as usual. Arthritis settled in his left hip and he walked in pain till the day he died. I felt bad for him. So I made the deal with God. I stopped—it stayed—so I continued to drink. I wondered if God really listened to our prayers.

Around this time I got involved at church with CYO—Catholic Youth Organization. I met other young Catholic teens whose faith was important to them. I found the courage to reach out to meet people I didn't know and I did it without alcohol! I even danced sober! My best friend Penny and I attended a CYO Convention. We had a blast! Then I attended a retreat called TEC—Teenagers Encounter Christ. I attended a workshop on 'Masks'—taking a look at the Masks we wear and being willing to take them off—to be more real. I began to find my true self, letting go of self-consciousness, and lightened up a bit. I felt loved and accepted by God and others on that weekend.

While my sisters were getting serious about guys, I still wasn't sure how I felt. Although I had dated a few boys, I still had crushes on girls. I had crushes when I was 4 or 5 years old. I didn't really understand it and hoped I'd outgrow it. But I didn't. I was anxious and confused. I dared not tell a soul. So I thought it would be best to check out this religious life thing. I always had a deep longing to feel closer to God, and serve His people, and this way I could avoid facing my sexuality and dating issues.

I secretly mailed in a post card that was on a Vocation's display at the back of church. I didn't want Mom and Dad to know. I was afraid they'd be too excited and then I'd be afraid to let them down if I changed my mind. As the information came in from various religious orders I did my best to get to the mail box before Dad. But eventually I told them. They were thrilled.

I attended a few vocation awareness weekends where I met other young people like myself who were interested in finding out more about religious life. I met Sisters and heard their stories about being called to Religious Life and how they decided to enter their specific religious community. I also learned why they call it Religious Life: if one lives according to that community's way of life one has a greater probability of becoming holy and of being closer to God. More specifically, going to daily Mass, receiving Holy Communion, praying the Divine Office two to three times a day and devoting an hour of your day to private prayer were conducive to creating the conditions where one would become a holy person. Those in Religious Life also attend annual retreats to deepen their spirituality and connection with God. For some, this way of life may feel like a chore, but to me, it was very appealing.

In the meantime, I was a scholar-athlete in high school, playing basketball and softball and making the honor society. I guess I was a junior when I developed an ability to hold my liquor. My boyfriend was very impressed. I loved the taste of whiskey and I had developed a taste for beer (chasers, anyone?). I considered myself a beer connoisseur, exploring beer from various countries. One day my boyfriend and I had just purchased Guinness Stout at the grocery

9

store (trying it for the very first time), and guess who walks in? Dad! He always seemed to catch me. A few years earlier at the age of 12 he caught me sneaking rum n coke at Penny's brother's eighth grade graduation. I had wanted to party like the older kids, only I was the one who got caught. Dad took me aside and told me how disappointed he was in me and that he had always trusted me. I felt awful. There was no need for additional punishment. I felt bad enough seeing the disappointment on his face and in his voice. Now here I was, four years later, caught again. Dad didn't say much this time, just teased us about trying Stout, but I knew not to come home drunk.

I partied through my two years of junior college, played sports and got mostly A's and B's. My college friends were looking at transferring to 4-year colleges. I didn't know what to major in and I couldn't get rid of the idea of becoming a nun.

 **Reflection**

Our past effects our present. Childhood experiences strongly influence who we have become. We each have a part of our parents within us, for good or not-so-good. Yet we can choose what parts we want to keep and which we want to let go of. It takes courage and strength to sort through it all.

Chapter 2

A Call to Religious Life

There's something cool about being a sister to everyone. It acknowledges our spiritual connection. The thought of living with a bunch of women actually sounded like fun! I'd also have the opportunity to improve my relationship with God through daily prayer, annual retreats, and by growing spiritually. All this sounded good to me. I was never much on worldly possessions. Material things have never had much impact on me. I was also never into fashion or the current trends. And although some of my best friends were men, I wasn't interested in dating them. Religious Life just seemed like a perfect fit. So I continued to visit religious communities in the area.

Then one day I got a call from Sister Mary Sunshine, who was from a Convent in Baltimore, Maryland. I had been corresponding with the vocation director, Sister Mary Wisdom, a few times through the mail. Receiving information through the mail was one thing, but a phone call seemed so serious and immediate! I was flabbergasted and yet excited. They were having a 'Live-In' weekend in a few weeks and I was invited. A 'Live-In' is where they invite a group of women, interested in religious life, for a weekend visit to take a closer look. I wasn't sure how far away it was or how I'd get there. Well, Sister Mary Sunshine was prepared! She already had bus information, which she shared with me over the phone. I checked with my parents and a plan was made to attend the 'Live In'. I'd get to experience their life-style first hand.

The day finally arrived. After a six hour bus ride Sister Mary Sunshine picked me up at the Greyhound bus station. She was a young sister with a bubbly personality. Sister asked how I was doing after the long bus ride. I was feeling tired and nervous, yet excited. "I'm terrific! Looking forward to the weekend!" I exclaimed, deciding to focus on the positive. We picked up another young woman at the Trailways bus station, and then we were on our way to the Convent.

It was a wonderful weekend. The Sisters were so warm and friendly. I enjoyed the Divine Office, which is a communal prayer based on Bible verses. The Sisters prayed the Divine Office three times a day: morning, noon and evening. The Office used the Psalms quite a bit. I always loved the Psalms. I find them very soothing. The Sisters prayed in two groups, alternating each verse, so as one group prayed in unison, the other group prayerfully listened. On Saturday night we had a party, Sister style. The Sisters dressed down in jeans and tee shirts (putting away their habits for the evening). We played games, ate popcorn and drank beer and soda. What struck me was that the Sisters drank beer out of the can! They were so REAL. I felt right at home. I had visited other communities but somehow knew I'd found my home here.

That summer I drove out to the Mother House in St. Louis with Sister Mary Sunshine and a couple other young women. I met more amazing nuns and really felt called to enter this community. I shared my decision with Sister Mary Wisdom, the vocation director. She was thrilled! Then I told my parents, over the phone, and they were excited for me as well. I'm sure they would have preferred that I had chosen a community closer to home, but they never said a word. They were very supportive.

I continued my last year at junior college, studying, attending a Christian prayer meeting once a week on campus, and began to wear a large cross around my neck. I had dated a very nice guy before I made the decision to enter the Convent and it was hard breaking up with him. I really cared for him and hated hurting his feelings. I figured wearing this cross would keep guys away. It seemed to work. I also played my last year of basketball and chose to play softball. There were parties with my team mates throughout the season. My decision to become a nun didn't change my desire to party. I figured I'd better get it out of my system while I had the chance.

During my sophomore year of college I flew out to St. Louis after Christmas to go through the application process. I took a battery of psychological tests and wrote my autobiography, which I read to the Sisters on the Formation Team. The Formation Team consisted of the Postulant Director, Sister Mary Celine, the Novice Director, Sister Mary Bernadette (Bernie for short), the Vocation Director, Sister Mary Wisdom, and the Temporary Professed Director, Sister Mary Patience. Each of these Sisters would play a role in my spiritual development. The purpose of the application process was to increase my self-awareness as well as help the Sisters get to know me better. We were laying the foundation for my journey of personal and spiritual growth, referred to as 'the Formation Process', which I would undergo upon entering the Convent.

The Sisters were kind and affirming as they challenged me to look at some of my issues before I entered that following September. Living in community, with a bunch of women, is not an easy task. It requires self-awareness and a willingness to grow. I became more acutely aware of my people pleasing tendency, which seemed to permeate everything I did. I was assured that the formation process would propel me forward in personal and spiritual growth. I welcomed this challenge, as I was young and eager to do God's will. I welcomed the Sisters' role in my growth and development. On September 8th, 1983, at the age of 20, I was to officially enter the community.

During my application process I met with Sister Mary Patience, who was a psychologist. I took a risk and shared with her a reoccurring dream that had been bothering me. In the dream I was kissing a woman. She asked "What do you think it means?" My face turned red. "I don't know." I couldn't find the courage to say what I thought it meant. She said it sounded like the dream was symbolic of my feminine side and my masculine side coming together as one. She encouraged me to focus on developing my femininity by wearing more feminine clothes, getting a purse and acknowledging my gentle side more. I was relieved!

When I returned to New York after being accepted to the Convent I went out bowling and drinking with my sister Carol and her friend. It was our usual custom to pick up some beer on the way to bowling. To celebrate this special occasion we got a few 6-packs Heineken and Molson—the good stuff—which we drank in the car before going bowling. It turned out to be league night so we never did bowl. But we talked and drank, as I told them about my experiences in St. Louis. The application process had increased my self-awareness. It felt good to share these insights with my sister Carol. We drank in the car in the parking lot, talked and listened to AC DC on the cassette player. To commemorate the occasion we made a Heine-Mol tree by placing some of our empty beer bottles on the branches of a small barren tree out in the parking lot.

My last semester of college sped by, marked by basketball games and parties, then softball games and more parties. I really enjoyed being part of a team. My two closest friends also played basketball. They were both Catholic and very supportive. I loved basketball and softball and hit my one and only grand slam while playing a team from Long Island. That was so cool!

Summer came and was filled with preparing for my departure to the Convent. Since I would be entering the Convent in September, my parents would drive me out to St. Louis the end of August. I tried to tone down the partying but was not very successful. My parents threw a going away party for me and asked me to be sure to watch my drinking. I was nervous about that. What if I got drunk at my own going away party?! That would be very embarrassing! I decided upon a strategy: I'd carry around my favorite New York Mets insulated cup, keep it filled with beer but drink it slowly by visiting with as many people as I could. Somehow it seemed to work. I was busy fielding questions about why I decided to become a nun. Many of my parent's friends thought that my parents pressured me into this. I assured them that I really did want to become a nun, to be a sister to all and to serve God in this way.

One night my parents were out. I was enjoying a few beers while playing cards in the kitchen with Carol and a couple of friends. As the evening progressed I realized I had more than a good buzz going. I realized I needed to get to bed before Mom and Dad came home. I didn't make it. All of a sudden I looked up and there they were, walking towards us. I was caught. I felt embarrassed. "How could I be drunk again? I'm going to become a nun, for God's sake!" I quickly said good night, hoping they didn't notice, but I was plagued with guilt. I needed to go to confession, but not to my parish priest. That would be too embarrassing.

I decided to go to Graymoor, which was about 30 minutes from my house. They had priests who heard confession on Saturdays at 4pm. I was very nervous as I walked into the 'face to face' confessional. I had opted for 'face to face' for years now and didn't want to hide-out behind a metal screen. I wanted to have a conversation, needing to clear my conscience and get some guidance. The priest was young, cool and 'with it'. He heard my story: entering the Convent soon; drank too much; nervous about leaving home. His advice: "Maybe you should take a look at your drinking. Sounds like you have an issue with alcohol." I assured him it was just due to the stress over this big change in my life. But he had planted a seed. I began to wonder if he was right.

The day came to say goodbye to Grandma and Grandpa and the rest of my family. I knew I'd see them in three months when I came home for Christmas. I was filled with mixed emotions. Sadness and excitement filled my soul. I left for the Convent with Mom and Dad and my two younger sisters, Tricia and Chris. We had a Midas Mini motor home. It made long trips more comfortable and convenient, with a bathroom on board. We packed it up and headed west to St. Louis, but first we did some sightseeing along the way. We camped in Hershey, PA, Amish Country, and then over to Baltimore, Maryland for a brief visit with the Sisters there, then finally turned our sights toward St. Louis, Missouri. We had a fun time together: riding the rollercoaster in Hershey Park, camp fires at night, family style dinners in Amish Country and photo ops with the Amish horse and buggy. For brief moments I forgot the purpose of the trip. We stopped periodically to refill our supply of beer, or should I say, my supply of beer. Mom and Dad were drinking their rum n cokes and at one point Dad commented on how fast I was going through the beer. I felt guilty and a little worried when I realized how nervous I was to be leaving home.

Finally, we arrived in St. Louis. Mom and Dad met the Sisters. We went sight-seeing with one of my classmates, who was a St. Louis native. We had a great time, until it was time for my family to head back to New York. We all cried. It was a hard to say good-bye.

Later that day, September 8th, 1983, my two classmates, Bonnie and Mary and I entered the Postulancy—from the Latin meaning 'to petition'—the first year of Religious Formation—the first step toward becoming a nun. The ceremony was simple. We were all so nervous! We had the giggles throughout the service, having a tough time saying our parts. But the Sisters were kind and understanding, remembering the day they entered as young postulants themselves. My adventure in religious life had begun!

 **Reflection**

Be curious. Be open. Be willing to follow your inner guidance. I believe for every problem there is a spiritual solution. We travel many paths in our lives. Each path has its own purpose, and offers the spiritual growth necessary for the next step. Life is a series of journeys, and each journey will bring us closer to Home, where we find our true connection with God.

Chapter 3

Getting Real

The first few weeks as a Postulant were very exciting. Everything was new! We lived in the Postulant house, which was a smaller house on the property. We lived separately from the other Sisters in order to learn how to live in community—to build community with each other. The 'We' included my two classmates, our Postulant Director, Sister Mary Celine, and me. The rest of the Sisters lived across the yard in the Big House, which was also the retreat center. We ate breakfast and lunch in the Postulant house and then had the evening meal at the Big House with the entire community.

This was my first Fall without being in school, though we did take a few classes on the vows and the history of the community. We had our daily chores at the retreat house. It was interesting and fun getting to know my classmates and the other Sisters.

As I mentioned earlier, we were in what was referred to as 'The Formation Process'. There are three stages in this process of becoming a nun. The first two stages consisted of the Postulancy, which lasted one year, and the Novitiate, which lasted two years. If we made it successfully through these stages we would petition to take temporary vows of 'Poverty, Chastity and Obedience' for one year. After that we would renew our vows each year for up to five years. At that point we would take perpetual vows or, if we realized that this way of life was not our calling, we would leave the community.

During the Postulancy we would build community with our director and our classmates and get to know the other Sisters. We would meet with our director weekly to further discern our call to religious life. By entering the convent we agreed to open ourselves to the formation team's feedback about areas where we needed to grow.

One day around lunch time I got a phone call from my sister Carol. I was so excited to hear her voice. "We just found out that Grandpa has liver cancer. The doctor gives him 6 months," Carol said. I was in shock. I got choked up and ended the call as quickly as I could. I was planning to go home for Christmas, so I'd see Grandpa in a couple of months. Sister Mary Celine, who was a nurse, told me what to expect. His skin and eyes would turn yellow jaundice as his liver began to fail. It would be hard to see him in this condition knowing he only had a short time to live. Once I worked through my denial about Grandpa's illness I felt intense anger. I wasn't used to feeling angry. I was angry with God and angry with cancer. I didn't know what to do with it. Sister Mary Celine told me that anger was a normal part of the grieving process. "God can handle your anger", she told me. She encouraged me to go out into the woods and scream "WHY?!?" as much as I needed in order to move through my grief. She also told me that beneath the anger was a deep sadness. Screaming "Why?" would allow me to release my hurt and sadness. It was a relief to know that what I was feeling was OK, and that it was alright to be angry with God.

A few weeks later, the tears started again, only this time I was homesick. I felt sad and empty inside. I hated to cry in front of people. I tried to hide it, but one look at my eyes and they could tell I'd been crying. I finally told Sister Mary Celine and my classmates what was up. They empathized and consoled me. They assured me it would pass. I got through it, and reached a new level of comfort in my new home and in my routine.

We were assigned various chores, including: cleaning the large Chapel in the Round, baking cookies for the retreatants and tending to the various gardens that surrounded the retreat house. We also participated on the high school retreats, which were led by Sister Liz.

I led small groups of high school seniors through various activities. I began to discover my leadership abilities and enjoyed facilitating small group discussion. We did an exercise where we made a 'Me-Bag' out of a large brown grocery bag. The idea was to cut out words and pictures from magazines and make a collage on the outside of the bag. The collage was a reflection of the 'You' that you show to the outside world. On the inside of the bag you put those things about yourself that were more personal and private—those things you only show to a select few. I wanted the teens to find me cool and approachable, so I put different beer ads on the outside of my bag. At one point it struck me how important beer was to my identity.

These retreats also made me keenly aware that speaking in front of the group brought on anxiety attacks. I'd break out in a sweat and hyperventilate. My voice shook and my heart pounded a mile a minute. I didn't know what to make of this.

We were supposed to spend an hour a day in prayer. We could pray in any way we chose: sit and do spiritual reading, meditate, sing, or pray in nature by taking a walk on the grounds and contemplate. I struggled with meditation. I really wanted to do it but would inevitably fall asleep. Sister Mary Sunshine had given a talk once about praying in nature and I really loved the idea. I love being outside. I grew up surrounded by woods and have always enjoyed the birds, the trees, the open sky and the quiet.

One day I took a walk out behind the retreat house, through the cow pasture and past the cows (did I mention the Sisters rented the land out to a rancher?) and out into the woods. I love deer. They are beautiful creatures. I asked God to please show me a deer. Off in the distance I saw two dogs. I got excited. I love dogs, too, so I called out to them. One of them started running toward me—galloping, actually. He was coming at me very fast, when I noticed he was growling. "Oh, Shit!" I fearfully exclaimed. "What do I do now?" I knew not to run. I turned and started to walk away quickly, looking over my shoulder as he kept coming toward me. I looked for a stick or rock to defend myself or for a tree to climb, but I found nothing.

He was getting closer when I imagined him shredding my legs—my legs all bloody. I went from fear to anger. He was about 10 feet from me when I screamed, "YOU GO HOME RIGHT NOW!!! YOU HEAR ME?!! GO HOME!!! GO HOME!!!" My blood was boiling—my heart racing. He stopped, growled, turned and walked a few steps in the other direction, then turned his head around at me and growled a few more times, then off he went, returning to the other dog and out of sight. The Utility Company was at the other end of the property, so I figured the dogs belonged to them. I calmed myself down, and continued walking. I still wanted to see a deer. I never did that day, but I learned a powerful lesson: I moved from being a victim to being empowered. I found my Power. I found my Voice, literally. And in doing so I saved myself from being chewed up by a wild dog! I stayed out of the woods for awhile after that. When I finally did return, I took with me a long, strong walking stick, just in case.

Part of the formation process is to learn about living the vows of 'Poverty, Chastity and Obedience'. The community I entered was very progressive, though they still wore the habit. We would listen to recorded talks on various topics. One such talk was given by a Sister who had given a workshop on sexuality and celibacy. She said that we're all sexual beings and that our desires do not automatically go away just because we've entered Religious Life. Though called to celibacy, she stated that "we are also called to be passionate lovers of God and people." Her statement enlightened my understanding of love and the natural desire for intimacy.

She also mentioned in her workshop how some people in religious life told her they were homosexual, as if to shock her. She told them that it didn't really matter, that all sexual feelings are natural and that what's important is what one chooses to do with those feelings. This information somewhat normalized my experience and helped me let go of the guilt I felt about being attracted to women. "I won't act on it, so what's the big deal?" I told myself.

During the evening meal at the Big House it became apparent that I didn't know how to socialize with the Sisters. I wasn't sure how to carry on a conversation. I felt like a fish out of water. They all joked around so easily. I, on the other hand, was self-conscious, quiet and serious. I'd always been that way, especially without alcohol. But now it appeared as if I was under a magnifying glass. My two classmates seemed to fit in. They were both playful, able to tease and joke around easily. I was raised to be courteous and I had difficulty being spontaneous. Excelling in sports, being a good student, drinking and partying were how I related. Put those things aside, I didn't know how to relate. What did I have to say? We didn't talk that much at home at the dinner table. How do adults socialize without alcohol? I wanted desperately to know the rules in order to blend in.

All these thoughts and feelings were bubbling to the surface. I didn't know how to deal with them so I tried to suppress them, hoping they'd go away. But then I began having strange, vivid dreams. In one of my dreams I was at the Convent, the Big House, and Dad was the dictator over the House. I felt controlled and angry. It was a very disturbing dream. I took my dream to Sister Mary Patience to help me figure it out. To my surprise, I realized just how angry I was with my Dad.

I loved my Dad, though he could be very controlling. I realized I was upset with him over many things, but most recently, I was upset with him over what I came to call 'The Tripe Incident'. The incident happened the summer before I entered the convent. We had company over: Grandma, Poppy and my two uncles. Mom put us to work making baked chicken and baked ziti. Our mouths were watering as we prepared the food. It was going to be delicious! Then Dad started to make a large pot of 'tripe soup' for his parents to enjoy. We'd never had *this* before. It smelled awful! One by one, as each kid passed through the kitchen, we'd innocently comment, "What's that horrible smell?" Poor Dad got his feelings hurt. He then made an announcement that the soup was now a required part of the meal, an appetizer. We had to eat it, or we didn't get the good stuff. As we all sat down to eat, the kids at one table, Carol and I at the adult table, everyone struggled with the soup. The kids had long faces, poking their spoons at the soup in their bowls. Finally Dad said, "Fine. If you don't want to eat it, pick up your bowls, put the soup back in the pot, and go downstairs. You're done with dinner." One by one, each of my siblings got up, put the soup back in the pot, and left the room, heading downstairs. "Oh, shit", I thought. I looked up, and then Carol did the same thing. Now, what was I going to do?!? I didn't want to eat it, but I wanted the chicken and baked ziti. I also didn't want Dad to be upset with me. So I forced myself to eat it. Somehow I finished my bowl of soup. Then I went for the chicken and baked ziti. The food was good, but would have been more delicious if not for my guilt.

After the meal I went downstairs to see how my Sibs were doing. "How was the chicken and baked ziti?" they all asked. "It was ok," I said, feeling like a traitor. I should have stood up to Dad, but I just couldn't. Later, Mom snuck them upstairs to eat some food while Dad was out for a walk. I realized I had a lot of anger to work through: anger with Dad, anger with Mom for not speaking up for us, and anger with myself.

I went home for Christmas. Poor Poppy was all yellow. No one told him he had cancer. I couldn't understand why. When he asked why he was turning yellow, Grandma told him he had a liver disorder. We weren't allowed to talk about the cancer in front of him. It felt weird. When I said good bye to him I wasn't sure if I'd ever see him again. I also noticed how much everyone drank. The house felt loud and busy. I longed for peace and solitude. I was looking forward to heading home—back to the Convent.

Life in the Convent continued. In the Spring we went through a communications class together. We learned how to talk about emotional issues as well as the nitty-gritty of community life. For example, being considerate when doing laundry; cleaning up after oneself; planning for grocery shopping together, etc. These were some of the things we learned to discuss openly and directly with each other. We learned the importance of using 'I' statements—being assertive—not passive nor aggressive.

In April I found out that Grandpa was in a coma. He didn't have much time. I asked the Sisters if I could go home to say goodbye. They told me that I could either go home now or wait until the funeral. I decided I needed to see him and say goodbye. My parents picked me up from the airport. I asked them how they were doing. "As best as can be expected, under the circumstances." They were stoic and silent. Grandma looked tired and sad. I gave her a big hug. She was happy to see me. When I saw my younger siblings, we were all able to talk about how sad we felt. They told me not to say a word about the cancer to Grandpa when I saw him. "Really? He still doesn't know he has cancer?" I asked. "No. We're not allowed to say anything to him or around him." Sometimes people in a coma can still hear what's going on around them, so we had to be careful about what was said.

It really bothered me that we still hadn't told Grandpa that he was dying. I figured it had to do with the denial of feelings that went on in my family. Many years later I learned why they kept it from him. Years before a friend of the family got sick with cancer. Grandpa told Grandma that if he ever got sick with cancer he would go out in the woods and shoot himself. Grandma and Dad were trying to prevent that from happening. But I didn't know this at the time. How was I supposed to say goodbye to him when I wasn't allowed to acknowledge the reality of the situation?

Finally we went to visit Grandpa in the hospital. My poor Poppy. He lay there as if asleep, all yellow, hooked up to an IV. I went over to him and gave him a kiss on the cheek. He just laid there. I told him it was me. "Hi Poppy. It's me, your Katharina. It's so good to see you." I held back the tears, put a smile on my face and tried to be cheerful for him and for my family in the room with me. "It's ok, Poppy. You just sleep now, get your rest." I felt like I was being monitored by my parents and by Grandma. "Keep up the facade. Don't let him know what's really happening."

After Mom, Dad and Grandma visited Grandpa at the hospital they went home and sat at the dining room table, staring into their rum n cokes, not saying a word. What was there to say? So much, yet it was too painful to put words to how we were feeling. It was easier to numb out. I felt the pressure—the tension. Over the past six months

I had a taste of healthy communication. This felt so uncomfortable. I needed relief from the tension, a break from the grief. I called my buddy Tommy and we went out to dinner. I had a few drinks, and they really hit the spot. I had a slight buzz and was feeling much better. When I came home that night I met Mom in the kitchen on her way to bed. It must have been around midnight. She was finishing up her last zip of rum n coke. She was feeling the effects of the alcohol, too. She said, "Oh, Kathy, I'm so happy you're here. It's so good to have you home." Then she held up her glass, "This is the only thing getting me through this." It was hard seeing Mom this way. I could see what this was doing to her and to my family, and why they were turning to alcohol. Ironically, I wasn't able to see that I was doing the very same thing.

The time came to say goodbye and return to St. Louis. I went to the hospital one more time to say goodbye to Grandpa. "I love you and I'll miss you, Poppy," I told him. My older sister Sue was a nurse at that hospital. I saw her on duty that day. We were both tearful as we hugged goodbye.

My friend Katie and her friend Laurie were waiting for me and took me out for a few beers before I left for the airport. They had already picked up a couple of sixes, so I opened one and started drinking as we drove off to the gorge, one of our favorite drinking places. The alcohol calmed me down and I stopped crying. I could tell that my friends felt uncomfortable with my tears as they tried to cheer me up. Before I knew it I was saying goodbye to Mom, Dad, Grandma, and my siblings. I headed back to St. Louis—back to my Convent life.

I don't remember who picked me up from the airport. When I got home no one was around. The next morning at breakfast Sister Mary Patience asked how my family was. "Fine", was all that I could say. "And your Grandpa?" I choked on my orange juice, couldn't stop coughing and left the room. I found a place to be alone and cried, then pulled myself together and went on with my day. Time passed slowly as I wondered how Poppy was doing. A few weeks passed. Then one morning, on the 1st of May, while I was answering the phones at the retreat center, Dad called. "Grandpa passed away early this morning. Grandma and I were there with him." "I'm so sorry, Dad," I tried not to cry. I sent my love to Grandma and Mom, and then quickly hung up the phone. I headed to the small bathroom just a few feet behind me, closed the door, sunk down on the floor and sobbed. My heart was aching. It felt like my heart and my insides were being ripped out. "I'll never see him again," I thought. Meine Liebe Poppy: the man who taught us the 'Schnitzelbank' song and who squeezed too hard when he hugged us; the man who drove Grandma crazy with his jokes, with his teasing and with his tricks; the man who fed wild birds out of the palm of his hand; the man who drank too much; the man I loved with all my heart.

"I can't keep this to myself. I need to tell someone", I thought. I washed my face and walked over to the Postulant house to find Sister Mary Celine. There she was in her office. Through my tears I told her that Grandpa died. She held me as I cried and said "I'm glad you came over to tell me." It was still hard to be real with my feelings. The Sisters and my classmates were empathetic and supportive. I had an exam that very evening in one of my classes. I wasn't sure I'd be able to concentrate but I pulled it off and did well. Later that week I called home after Poppy's funeral mass. I spoke with my sisters. They were all partying, toasting Grandpa and reminiscing about the good times. "Grandpa wouldn't want us to cry. He'd want us to celebrate his life. Have a beer on Grandpa!" I wished I was there. But then I was glad I wasn't.

I met monthly with Father John for spiritual direction. During my session I shared what had happened when I was home saying goodbye to Grandpa. I told him how we didn't talk about Grandpa dying nor about our feelings, and how I wished we had. He said, "Maybe you should talk with your family when you go home this summer. It would be good to grieve together." I thought it was a great suggestion, and planned to do that during my next home visit.

25

 **Reflection**

Though I didn't know it at the time, my Grandpa's illness and death were powerful catalysts for change. Change is rarely easy, seldom welcome and yet is often necessary for growth. During the transition from old to new, we tend to be off balance. Patience is the key. With time you will adjust to the new and regain your footing. Have faith in the process of life.

Chapter 4

Hitting Bottom

It was finally time for my home visit. I had 2 weeks to enjoy my family. My two oldest sisters, Sue and Carol, were now married and living in their own homes. I tried to find time to share with them, but it seemed that drudging up feelings about Grandpa's death wasn't a top priority. Sue was busy with her new husband and it seemed that my visits with Carol usually revolved around partying. I wasn't complaining. It felt good to party again. At the Convent I'd have a few brews with the Sisters at picnics or while watching the Cardinals play baseball. Although I did hide a small bottle of Jack Daniels in my room to increase my buzz, nothing was quite like partying unencumbered with my own sisters, out in the open, with the intention of numbing out, getting a good buzz. I knew that getting drunk was a sin, so I was trying to control myself. But once I started I never knew when I would stop. I didn't have much control over the 'stopping' aspect.

One night at Carol's apartment, after drinking quite a bit, her friend Karen needed a ride home. She had her little daughter with her. Carol thought I was alright to drive, so she asked me to drive Karen home. I was too embarrassed to tell Carol that I was too drunk to drive. I tried to sober up by thinking of the possible consequences of driving drunk. I mustered as much clarity as I could and carefully drove them home. I got there and back, safe and sound. PHEW!

Another night, after we'd been drinking at Carol's, someone passed around a joint. I didn't smoke because it burned my lungs. But I was always curious about pot and what being 'high' felt like. I had a nice buzz, so I took a drag. I didn't feel the burn, so I took another. I smoked enough to get the giggles. My younger sister, Tricia, and I left for home. We both had the munchies. We warmed up some of Grandma's delicious lasagna and headed out to the pool deck. We had a great time eating and giggling.

At one point my friends came by, already high. I was jealous they hadn't waited for me. Then I saw how silly they acted, and thought, "I looked like THAT? I'm not smoking pot anymore." But I still hung out with them quite a few times while I was home for those two weeks. I got pretty wasted on beer and shots of peppermint Schnapps. It was a bad combination. The room was spinning as I tried to fall asleep that night. I stared at the alarm clock, trying to make the room stop spinning. It would work for a few seconds, but before long, the room would start spinning again.

I never did talk with my family about Grandpa's death. I never grieved with them. It never seemed like the right time. And we were always too busy partying. By the time I returned to the Convent I had lost count of how many times I'd gotten drunk in those two weeks. Even worse, I defended myself by thinking I was just letting loose, having fun with old friends. Although I felt guilty about being drunk, smoking pot, and losing control, I wanted more. I especially wanted to smoke more pot. I liked being high and having the giggles. I began plotting how I could acquire some without getting caught. I thought of asking Carol to mail some to me. Then I wondered what the legal consequences would be if we got caught. So I thought I'd see if someone locally could get some for me. Jan worked in the kitchen and we had become friends. I was tempted to ask her, but didn't. Then I suddenly realized what I was doing. "Am I crazy? First of all, it's illegal. Secondly, I'm in a Convent. Thirdly, Sister Liz would kill me if she found out. I'd feel terrible betraying her trust." I remembered how Sister Liz would tell the high school seniors who were coming to our retreat center (and home), "Don't bring any alcohol and none of those funny cigarettes." We all laughed. How could I even think of violating our home and Sister Liz's wishes? What was wrong with me?!?

Bonnie and I entered the Novitiate in August. Mary had decided to leave the previous spring, realizing she no longer felt called to Religious Life. Bonnie and I attended an intercommunity class with other Novices. Our teachers were usually Sisters from different communities. We learned about scripture, prayer, celibacy and living in community. 'Silence' was a topic spoken about in the prayer course. "When you get in the car, don't turn on the radio right away. Give yourself time for silence. Become aware of the chatter in your mind. When you can quiet your mind and be in the silence, you then have an opportunity to know God," one teacher taught us. I was getting better at silence. Sometimes I actually craved it. At other times I ran from it. It was too difficult to be alone with my thoughts.

As novices, Bonnie and I moved into the Big House (retreat house). We joined second year Novice, Nancy, in the Novitiate Wing along with Sister Mary Bernie, our Novice Director. Nancy was an Apostolic Novice who taught at a Catholic inner city grade school. She spent most of the week at our smaller house with the temporary professed Sisters who were attending college at St. Louis University.

The Big House could be rather lonely. After dinner some Sisters hung out in the community room, watching TV. The younger, 'cooler' Sisters would go to the solarium, light a fire in the fireplace and visit together. I wanted to be with the 'cool' group, but always felt on the outside looking in, a flash back from my childhood. It was tough walking into the solarium. Even when I forced myself to walk in, I felt very self-conscious. They all seemed to like Bonnie more than me. Bonnie was fun and spontaneous. I hung out with Nancy when she was home on the weekends. We got along well since we were both quiet and reflective.

It was a Friday night during the last week of September. I had gone to my room after dinner. I tried to pray. I thought about Poppy and all that happened while I was home before he died. It was so painful, seeing him that way, and it was painful how isolated we all were from each other. I missed him, and started crying. I couldn't stop. I went to Sister Mary Bernie's room for comfort and support. I started to knock on her door, but then decided not to disturb her. It was around 8:30pm. Maybe she was praying.

29

I left the building to take a walk in the dark. As I walked around the front of the Retreat House I looked for a place to sit. I found a tree and sat beneath it and sobbed, pulling my knees into my chest. My heart was aching. I couldn't stop crying. I was a blubbering mess. All the pain I had bottled up over the past five months came gushing out. How I longed to connect with my family about this. "I hate this!" I thought to myself. One minute I felt angry—at God, at cancer, at my folks—then the next minute I was incredibly sad. "This whole thing just sucks." As much as I hated to admit it, I knew I needed to get these feelings out. I sat out there crying until I couldn't breathe through my nose. It was late. I was exhausted and decided to go back inside.

I went back to my room, washed my face, brushed my teeth, changed into my pajamas and went to bed. I quickly fell asleep. The next day I told myself "You did good. You felt your feelings without medicating them with alcohol. Good Job! Now you deserve a break." I asked Nancy if she wanted to go to a movie that evening. We made our plans and, after dinner, we took off. We both enjoyed beer, so we got a six pack and shared it in the car before the movie. I told her what had happened the night before and how I'd been feeling. She was very caring and concerned as she listened to my story. Feeling "feelings" was not an easy task for either of us. With her understanding I felt less alone.

 **Reflection**

Do not be afraid to go through pain. Pain—emotional pain—can be a good motivator for change and growth.

Chapter 5

Getting Sober

Sunday came and I was one step closer to my weekly meeting with Sister Mary Bernie. I felt nervous about telling her what happened Friday night. Monday arrived. Sister Mary Bernie and I met outside in the sunshine, outside the Postulant house. People on retreat were walking the grounds, some within hearing distance of us. I didn't feel comfortable opening up to her out here. I was afraid I would cry. "Can we talk inside?" Sister Mary Bernie agreed, wondering what was up with me. We moved into the conference room in the Novitiate wing. "I have something to tell you," I said. I wasn't sure where to start. "I was crying Friday night. I cried so hard that I couldn't stop." "Why didn't you come and get me?" she asked. "I didn't want to disturb you," I said. "All the feelings I'd stuffed around my Grandpa's death . . . when I was home saying goodbye to him . . . all the pain came to the surface." I told her about the lack of communication, about the drinking to cope with the pain. Of course, I didn't mention my own drinking.

After I explained what it was like when I was home saying goodbye to Grandpa, Sister Mary Bernie said, "Kathy, do you think your parents are alcoholic?" I said, "I don't know," which became my default response to anything I didn't want to look at. Sister Mary Bernie gave me a book to read, 'Adult Children of Alcoholics', by Janet Woititz. "Read this and we'll discuss it later in the week. You may not relate to all of it. Focus on what you do relate to," she said.

Sister Mary Bernie was right. There were many things I didn't relate to—like coming home to a drunken Mom, passed out in the living room—but I did relate to the feelings. I wasn't comfortable in my own skin. I didn't know how to think for myself. I didn't know how I felt. In the book I saw these words: 'Don't Talk—Don't Trust—Don't Feel'—the unspoken rules of an alcoholic family. Here in the Convent I had felt like a fish out of water. I was beginning to find my pool. Though this was just a beginning, it was a relief to know there was a name for what I'd been experiencing.

Sister Mary Bernie found a family program for me to attend to help me learn more about alcoholism and how I had been affected by it. I was nervous about attending, yet knew I needed to do this. The first day, when we all shared why we were there, I told the group about my parents and my grandparents' drinking. I listened to other family members' experiences as they shared their feelings. I met their 'significant other' in treatment—real live alcoholics—and I began to compare notes with them. Man, could I relate. I recalled tasting a 7n7 on the basketball court in the middle of a game. I was craving it. I told them about getting drunk when I only intended to get a nice buzz. I realized that when I drank it was like playing Russian Rolette: once I started I didn't know when I would stop. I had lost the ability to control my drinking. Would I get drunk this time or not? Could I drive home safely? By the end of the week I told the group, "I think I may be an alcoholic." They were all supportive. The counselor told me that she'd ask her friend, a recovering alcoholic, to take me to an AA meeting if I'd like. I was willing.

Weeks went by, and that meeting never happened. I guess her friend was out of town. I was getting antsy. I wasn't drinking but, boy, did I want to. With the support of Sister Mary Bernie, Bonnie and my Aftercare group, I decided to go to a beginners' AA meeting. After dinner I went alone to what I thought was the address. I walked into this building but couldn't find the meeting. There were two men in the hallway. "Hi. I'm looking for the AA meeting. Do you know where it is?" I asked. "Why are you going to an AA meeting? You're too young to be an alcoholic. We're heading out for a drink. Why don't you join us?" they said. "No thanks. Do you know where the meeting is?" They directed me to the building across the parking lot. I left them quickly, heading across the lot to the meeting before I had a chance to talk myself out of it.

It was December 4, 1984, the day I walked into my first AA meeting. I looked around the room and found a seat. The room was crowded with people. The meeting had already started. Someone was reading something. Then the speaker told his story. He described the chaos his drinking caused in his life. I'd never had a car accident, never gotten a DUI, and never lost a job, so I couldn't relate to his low bottom. But I identified with his patterns of drinking and with his feelings. "Damn It! I am an alcoholic," I later wrote in my journal. "I will not drink today, for it is always today. God, I'm scared! Help me please!"

When I arrived back at the Big House I looked for Sister Mary Bernie. I ran into Bonnie and told her I'd gone to my first AA meeting. She was happy for me. Then I found Sister Mary Bernie in the kitchen. "How was the meeting?" she asked. "Good," was all that I could muster, my mind still processing what I'd heard at the meeting. "What do you think? Are you an alcoholic?" "Yes, I think so . . . but maybe I can drink a little and just not get drunk," my denial flaring up. "That would be 'sober', right?" I thought to myself. "Kathy, if you don't stop drinking, you can't stay here," Sister Bernie said plainly. "Oh . . . I see." The seriousness of my predicament was sinking in. I didn't want to leave. I had to stay honest with myself. If I wanted to grow, to change, and if I wanted to stay here, I had to continue to choose sobriety and say 'Yes' to living. I prayed in my journal two days later "Please, help me—give me the strength and courage to keep battling off my denial and rationalizations. I don't want to be a mess. I want to be happy and free."

There was so much churning inside of me that I just couldn't talk to Sister Mary Bernie about. It felt too scary to bring up my issues with my Aftercare group. There was a counselor who some of the Sisters were seeing named Sister Carol. I had taken a class with her the previous semester. She seemed knowledgeable and approachable. I told Sister Mary Bernie I really needed to start counseling with Sister Carol. She agreed and gave me permission to call for an appointment. I prayed to God that Sister Carol had an opening and would be able to see me soon. I was relieved when I called and she was able to schedule an appointment the following week. As we met I shared my family history and my struggle with staying sober. She was very supportive and understanding. It turned out that she had also been raised in an alcoholic family and was recovering by attending Al-Anon meetings on a regular basis. She understood the disease and the importance of attending AA meetings for long term sobriety. I found a weekly AA meeting to attend and started to get familiar with the 12-Steps.

I always felt close to my family, but now I wasn't sure what to tell them when we spoke on the phone. I longed to tell them everything I was going through, but I sensed they wouldn't understand. However, I was able to tell my sister Carol about it. She agreed that alcoholism ran in our family. She could see it. But when I told her we had a 90% chance of becoming alcoholic, because it was on both sides of our family, she was skeptical. "Carol, I think I'm alcoholic," I tested the water to see where she was at. "You? No, come on, Kath. You may overdo it sometimes, but you're not an alcoholic."

It wasn't safe to tell her more, that I *knew* I was an alcoholic. When I hung up the phone my denial was rearing its ugly head. I had to remind myself of what I knew: that once I started drinking I couldn't predict when I'd stop and that alcohol was not only an issue for me but for my family. I was learning to speak a new language—a language that included words like 'alcoholism' and 'honesty'—a language my family didn't speak nor understand.

I began to tell myself "It's inevitable that I'll drink again, so why not just do it and get it over with?" But then I remembered all the pain that alcoholism had caused and how I wanted to grow, to change and be free. I hated alcoholism. I hated how manipulative I was in relating with people, doing or saying what I thought they wanted to hear to ultimately get my way. I wasn't even sure whether I wanted to stay sober for myself or to please others. I guess it was a little of both. Sister Carol assured me that it really didn't matter why I was staying sober, as long as I did and continued to go to my AA meetings. I guess she figured eventually I'd stay sober for myself.

The Oblates of Mary novices hosted a Halloween party. I went and had a great time visiting with the other novices that I'd met in class. I stayed sober during the party and discovered that it wasn't really all that difficult! I even felt outgoing and enjoyed dancing with everyone, all without the buzz of alcohol. I felt proud of myself. I could stay sober and had fun. I realized that alcohol had become my Higher Power. I wanted God to be the center of my life. I began to see staying sober as a moral issue.

My success at the Halloween party quickly lost its power and the clarity of that 'Aha' moment in October was fading. With each new day came the struggle to stay sober. I was preoccupied with drinking and I was irritable. As a Canonical Novice my involvement with the outside world was to be very limited. Because of this the Sisters allowed me to attend only one AA meeting a week, and one meeting a week was just not cutting it.

One evening I was sitting in the little chapel in the Novitiate wing, craving a beer. Cans of Busch and Coors were sitting in the small refrigerator down the hall by the Solarium and they were calling my name. I'd heard at an AA meeting to pray for the desire not to drink. I wanted to drink so badly that I prayed for the desire TO DESIRE *not* to drink. In that moment, the craving lifted and I was at peace. That peaceful feeling remained with me the rest of the night.

When I woke up the next day the desire to drink was waiting for me once again. If this is beginning to sound redundant, that's exactly how it felt. I couldn't escape. I was at war within myself. I wanted to stay sober. I wanted to honor my sobriety date as well as my commitment to God. And yet I wanted to have one good last drunk, to hit a bottom so low that the pain of it would propel me into a stronger sobriety. I turned to God in prayer, asking for God's help, and that prayer brought relief. Day by day I continued to vacillate: wanting sobriety—wanting to drink. The struggle was SO *exhausting*. Bonnie suggested that I write down my drinking history. I did so and my denial weakened. I began to gain the clarity of truth: I was truly powerless over alcohol. Once I started to drink I could not predict when I'd stop. So it wasn't safe for me to take a drink. I told myself "to drink is to die, and to drink is to invite chaos into my life."

At Christmas time the Sisters were given gifts of wine and alcohol, dressed in beautiful bottles. They put them on a table in the solarium for all the Sisters to share. One night everyone was hanging out in the solarium. I couldn't walk in there and face the alcohol or the Sisters. I wanted to be alone, so I went to our small community room to journal. I wanted to disappear and make all this go away. Sister Mary Bernie came in. "What are you doing in here all by yourself? Why don't you join us?" "I can't be around all that alcohol," I said. She was disappointed yet tried to understand. She decided to look into treatment options for me. She found an inpatient program with an excellent reputation, and asked if I'd be open to meeting with a counselor there. I couldn't continue like this, so I agreed.

I was quiet as we drove to the appointment. We met the counselor, a young woman, slightly older than me. "She's friendly and seems very happy, for being an alcoholic," I thought. She spent a lot of time talking about herself. She shared her story. "When is she going to ask about me?" I wondered. Then she said, "So, Kathy, are you an alcoholic?" "Yes, I am," I said. "Do you think you need treatment?" "I don't know. I'm really not that bad," I told her. After all, I'd stayed sober for almost three months—never mind I was in a living hell. She said, "When I entered treatment I had a beautiful house, a wonderful family and two cars in the garage. How bad does it have to get?" My denial broke. She had me. It could always get worse. Even though it didn't look bad on the outside, it was bad on the inside. I agreed to go into treatment.

Once home we shared the news with other Sisters. Sister Mary Patience told me I was psychologically strong enough to benefit from treatment and encouraged me to be open and to give my all to the treatment experience. Though I doubted her words, it was reassuring to hear her say that. My insides felt fragile and ready to crumble. It was early January, 1985. Sister Mary Bernie drove me to the Treatment Center to be admitted. She helped me get settled in my room. I sat there staring at the floor, feeling like a lost little girl. She saw how scared I was and walked over to give me a hug. I sensed her concern, as if she was worried about my ability to deal with this. I hugged her back, reassuring her that I'd be ok.

I had been dry for three months and I didn't want them to put me on 'detox' meds. I worked so hard to *keep* my sobriety date—October 1, 1984—and I didn't want to lose it, especially over detox meds!!! They took my vitals. They were good, within normal limits. No detox was needed. The first few days I attended lecture, had meals with the group and just hung around with everyone. When they went to group I was left alone. I visited with the nurses, but I was getting bored. "When will I get to meet with my counselor and go to group?" I wondered. Then I heard from another patient that they didn't really engage him in treatment for about a week. He figured they wanted him to get bored and ready for treatment. I was ready already! Let's get on with it!!

Finally my counselor Bill came into my room. "Ready to party?" he said. "Yeah . . ." unsure what he meant. "How do we party in here", I thought. "Let's go to group." He led the way to the meeting room. There was a small group of about eight patients in the room, sitting in a circle. I introduced myself, telling them why I was here. Then Bill opened up the session in his usual way, "This is your group. Who wants to start?" Then we sat in silence. Finally someone brought up an issue around their addiction. In active addiction many things get overlooked and left unsaid. There were a lot of situations to address, but newly sober addicts/alcoholics don't open up very easily. I knew I'd have Sister Carol to talk to after treatment, so I wasn't sure what to bring up in group.

I met with Bill to go over an assessment to determine my diagnosis. I was paranoid that he'd discover I wasn't alcoholic, that I really didn't belong here. If I didn't belong here, where did I belong? I wasn't bad enough and he'd find out I was an imposter. I so longed to know for sure I belonged *somewhere* and that there was something wrong with me that could be treated and fixed. To my relief, he did diagnose me as chemically dependent, in the beginning stages of addiction, 'primordial stage' I think he called it. "You're an over achiever. You stopped your addiction much sooner than most," Bill told me. I think it would have pleased him to see me rebel a bit.

37

The program was based on the 12 Steps of Alcoholics Anonymous, which I had been introduced to at my AA meetings. We had to work the first 5 Steps in order to graduate the program. Of course, we'd continue to work the remaining 12 Steps after treatment by attending AA meetings and working with a sponsor. But while in treatment your counselor gave you a Hazelton guide filled with questions regarding each step. You had a few days to work that step by reading the guide and completing the questions.

Step One talked about being powerless over alcohol. I wrote in detail how I was powerless over my drinking and how alcohol brought chaos into my life. The guide also asked the question: "What is the difference between 'admitting' and 'accepting'?" The other patients were an invaluable resource in working the steps. They helped me answer the question correctly. "To admit is done mostly in the mind. It's a logical thing. To accept is done more deeply, and it's more on a feeling level." That felt right, so I wrote it down.

The 2nd and 3rd Steps addressed coming to find a Power Greater than oneself. Spirituality came easily to me. I knew there was a God. I couldn't prove it and didn't need to. I felt it. I turned to God many times. But how could I do it consistently in order to stay sober? How could I do it in every area of my life? I hadn't a clue. Then I was reminded that we do it 'One Day at a Time'. I was also reintroduced to the Serenity Prayer. I remembered we had the Serenity Prayer hanging on our dining room wall, but I didn't really know what it meant. I began to learn its true meaning and felt an instant connection with each verse. It has become a spiritual tool I've used often through the years.

I met a lot of nice people in treatment. We played Trivial Pursuit every night after the evening lecture. I moved into a new room and got a new roommate named Barbara. Barbara was very sweet. She was from Arkansas and spoke with an accent. I loved her accent. It wasn't long before I was speaking with an accent.

Barbara shared something her counselor had taught her. We were talking about the 3rd Step of AA—turning our lives over to God's care.

Barbara was holding a box of tissues. "Here's my life. Take it." She handed the box over to me, but didn't let go. "Take it," she said again, attempting to hand it to me, still holding on. Then she tossed it to me. "Here. Have it." I caught the box. "That's how you turn it over," she said. I got it, but doing it would take many years of practice.

It was snowing one night. We weren't allowed outdoors after the 7pm Lecture. Pat, my new buddy, loved the snow. He just HAD to be out in it. So he led a few of us out the side door, propping it open ever so slightly so as to not lock ourselves out. We ran around in the dark playing in the snow. We had so much FUN! We had snow ball fights and made snow angels. It was a magical night. We got back in without being caught. For this we could have been thrown out of treatment. What dare devils we were!

One day a new patient named Alice was admitted to our unit. Alice was an ex-nun and an out Lesbian. I didn't know any Lesbians and found myself intrigued. She had gone through the two week Family Program. During that time she admitted she was alcoholic. Some of the Family Program alumni took her out the night before treatment for her final night of drinking. She came into treatment pretty hung over. I was jealous. Part of me still wished I'd had a last 'hurrah', one deliberate, final drunk. But then again, I might have never stopped.

Alice and I became friends. One day I told her, "I'd probably be Gay if the Catholic Church approved of it." She was a rebel. She didn't follow the official teachings of the Catholic Church anymore. I wished I could be as free. But I was too concerned about the opinion of others, including the Catholic Church.

I called Mom and Dad to tell them where I was. They were shocked. After I told them I was alcoholic, I told them I was concerned about their drinking too. Their denial was clear in their response, "No, Kathy. That can't be. You're not alcoholic, and neither are we." I tried not to let their denial affect me. I pressed on with my own treatment. I was aware of my denial as it came up, seeing it more clearly in my parents than in myself at times. I had really hoped they'd see the light of truth, but that wasn't the case. The distance grew between us. I was very sad and disappointed.

Sister Carol came for a brief visit. We had barely begun the therapy process before I came into treatment. She encouraged me to learn all I could about my disease and to be open to direction from my counselor. I learned a lot. I learned that alcoholism tends to run in families; and that it's a disease, just like diabetes. You must abstain in order to arrest the disease, but you're never cured of it. I also learned that I must abstain from all mood altering chemicals otherwise I'd have a good chance of becoming addicted—that I could change my drug of choice. The shame of addiction began to lift as I accepted these concepts. When others realized I was in the Convent, preparing to become a nun, they felt better about being addicted too. "If a nun can be an alcoholic, I guess I'm not so bad."

When it came time to write my 4th Step I was very honest. In the 4th Step I needed to take a look at my behavior and how I've violated my own values due to my drinking. I wanted to let go of my regrets, my guilt and shame; to leave it there at the Treatment Center and be free. Once I wrote my 4th Step I would share it with the minister on staff. This is called giving your 5th Step. The minister was young, with a great sense of humor. I told him that, due to my drinking, I didn't live up to my values. For example, I was a huge advocate of not littering, yet when I drank beer while driving I threw beer cans out the window into the woods, in an effort to get rid of the evidence. I unloaded my guilt about sneaking alcohol, and driving drunk; unloaded the shame I felt over peeing my pants while vomiting after partying with friends in the woods, and then walking around town with soiled jeans. Yes, drinking led to many embarrassing moments. In the light of addiction and forgiveness, I was letting it go and slowly becoming free. After giving my 5th Step, I bundled up and went outside to the metal box, which was shaped like a 4, and burned my 4th Step, as was the tradition. A small group of friends witnessed it with me. It was freeing to let it go.

As I prepared to leave I passed around my AA Big Book and had everyone sign it. I said my goodbyes. I'd be back weekly for my evening aftercare group. I hoped to see my new friends again there or at AA meetings. My counselor, Bill, led me out to the reception area where Sister Mary Bernie was waiting for me. "Before you go, I have something to show you. Come with me," Bill said. I followed him back to the business office where he showed me the bill for my treatment. I was shocked to see that the bill came to around $8,000. The Sisters paid the co-pay of about $500. "See this?" Bill said. "You pay this back by staying sober. Take responsibility for your recovery, One Day at a Time." I understood and felt so grateful to the Sisters for helping me get sober.

I settled back into Convent life. I was lonely, not having my new friends to hang out with. But I felt grateful for my sobriety. The Sisters were all busy during the day doing their jobs. I was assigned to organize the library. One day while sorting through some books I discovered a copy of The Serenity Prayer. I'd heard there was a long version and here it was! It is such a beautiful prayer. I tried to memorize it, but it was too long. So one day I grabbed my guitar, and miracle of miracles, I wrote music to it. I figured if I could sing it, I'd remember it. I memorize songs rather easily. The song sounded so pretty. I sang it often, to remind myself how to approach life: 'Accept the things I can't change'—my alcoholism, other people—'Change the things I can'—choosing to stay sober; choosing to grow and become the best person I can possibly be—'Wisdom to know the difference'—Asking God for help in sorting it all out.

I went to my Aftercare group each Wednesday evening. When that meeting was finished I went back to the unit to visit with my friends. One night I lost track of time and got home late. The next day I got grounded—grounded for coming home too late!! I'd never been grounded in my entire life! Now I got grounded in the Convent! Holy Shit! I sure knew how to get into trouble. It reminded me of when I got in trouble when was about 13 yrs old. I brought the Sheriff to our front door. I was walking with my friend Penny along a two lane highway. She told me to toss a snowball onto a car that was driving by. I flicked the snowball into the air. It fell on the roof of the car, and then it crumbled down onto the windshield. The driver hit the brakes. We panicked. We ran and hid under the nearby bridge.

After several minutes we looked up and there he was, looking down at us. "Hey, you kids, get up here." He turned out to be an off duty Sheriff's Deputy. His kids were in the car and were shaken up when he hit the brakes. I could have caused an accident. I felt horrible. "Expect a visit from the Sheriff," he said after he asked for my name. When the Sheriff arrived at my house, Dad answered the door. I was downstairs in the play room. Dad came down and found me. "Do you know who's in our drive way? Look out the window." Dad said. There was the Sheriff's car. Dad was angry, embarrassed and very disappointed in me, but I didn't get grounded. I guess it was about time I experienced the consequences of my actions.

Inter-Novitiate classes started back up again mid January. I met a few new novices who hadn't participated in the last course. I quickly developed a crush on one young woman who had also gone through the same treatment center. We had a lot to talk about. She took the morning class only. I had a full day of classes. One day I saw her shooting baskets out in the yard. I skipped class to spend time with her. I just loved the 'high' of infatuation. But with the high came the guilt for feeling this way. I'd learned that feelings are feelings and your body doesn't know that you're choosing celibacy. Choosing religious life and celibacy doesn't mean you can't develop friendships or even fall in love, but you choose to remain celibate. "Ok," I thought. "It's just a crush. It'll pass. I must be more in the 'Bi' region. I'm called to celibacy, so I can't do anything about it anyway." I tried to reassure myself. But I couldn't stop thinking about her in a romantic way.

One day in late February, Sister Mary Bernie and Sister Mary Wisdom confronted me during my weekly meeting. "You're in a dry drunk," they said. I was dumbfounded. I thought I was doing great with my sobriety. Being an over-achiever and a people pleaser, I intended to do the very best I could at this 'recovery' thing. Being told that I was in a dry drunk made me feel guilty and ashamed. "You're not being honest about something. You seem withdrawn. We suggest you talk with Sister Carol about whatever is going on with you." Then I realized what it was. My skipping class and fantasizing about 'her' was not appropriate. I decided to be honest with Sister Carol about what was going on with me.

Sister Carol laid it on the line. "There's nothing wrong with your feelings. But there is something wrong with being dishonest. Skipping class and lying about it are not ok." I knew that. I had to stop being sneaky. It has become such a habit. I'd learned to be sneaky growing up around my Dad. He was very controlling, though his intentions were good. He made us wear a belt with our jeans, despite the fact that it wasn't the cool thing to do at my high school. He told us what movies we could see, based on a monthly newsletter of movie reviews by the Catholic Bishops. We'd pick a movie that was approved, then went out and saw what we wanted to anyway. Being sneaky was a hard habit to let go of.

It was sometime in April, 1985, when I found myself daydreaming about being single, having my own apartment, a job and dating. Then I thought, "Would I date men or women?" Realizing what I was thinking, I shut myself down. "Oh, Shit! This is too scary!" and back into denial I went. I looked around and saw where I was, in the hallways of the Convent. I must have done this several times, when suddenly it hit me, "OMG! I'm in a Convent. I'm taking vows in August! What am I doing here?" I learned in AA that God's Will for us is to be 'Happy, Joyous and Free'. Wearing a skirt and nylons everyday was not my idea of 'Happy, Joyous and Free'. What was I going to do?

Around this time I had another vivid dream. I was driving the Vocation Director's car, following my big sister Sue, who was in a car ahead of me. Sue turned left but I kept going straight. I was going too fast to make the turn to follow her. Over and over I drove the same road, trying to catch up with her, and repeatedly I missed the turn, as I was unable to slow down.

Then one day Sister Mary Bernie and Sister Mary Wisdom sat me down and told me they wanted me to take a leave of absence for a year or two in order to get my recovery stronger and further discern if I still had a call to be a nun. They saw that I was struggling. I was shocked and yet relieved: shocked in that I had failed at becoming a nun; relieved in that I wasn't sure I really wanted to do this. Now

43

my dream made sense: my vocation was going too fast. I needed to slow things down. I needed more time.

The Sisters didn't want me to go home to New York. They were afraid that I'd relapse if I went back to live with my family. I was afraid of that too. They wanted me to be close by so Sister Mary Bernie and I could meet monthly to continue to discern my vocation. The Sisters looked for a family who could take me in and help me find a job and get on my feet. It took a couple of months, but they finally found one. During that waiting period it was tough being with the Sisters. They all knew I'd be leaving soon and started to distance themselves from me. I felt very lonely and was growing impatient to move on. Finally a home surfaced. Eric and Jen took in young women who were trying to get their lives on track. I'll bet they never dreamed they'd be helping an ex-nun!

 **Reflection**

Getting sober was one of the hardest things I'd ever done. It required total honesty. It turned my world upside down. And yet it was the greatest gift I've ever given to myself. Though my alcoholism was arrested early, it did affect those around me, especially the Sisters. They cared enough to intervene, to put me through treatment, to find a family for me to stay with so I could continue my recovery. It cost them greatly, and for their generosity I am eternally grateful.

Chapter 6

Life After the Convent

In early September, 1985, I left the Convent and moved in with Eric and Jen and their two daughters. I had a room in the basement with my own bathroom. Eric was the director of pastoral care at a local hospital. Jen ran a day care center. Eric was also a great mechanic. He helped me find a used car, a 1976 Audio Fox, a two door, 5 speed stick. It had some rust but it was mechanically sound. When I was about 16 my Uncle Tommy taught me how to drive a stick, so I was able to handle this car. It was sporty with a lot of pep. I loved it! The Sisters loaned me $500 to buy it and I paid them back, $100 monthly. Soon it would be all mine!

Eric helped me get a job at the hospital as a phlebotomist. They needed someone part time to help out on the early morning shift when most of the blood draws were done. I'd never drawn blood before and actually hated hospitals, but I took the job. The staff trained me. I was what we jokingly called a 'vampire.' I worked from 5-9 am, came home and visited with Jen, helping her with the kids. Then Jen got a request to take in a three year old boy. She asked if I wanted to take the job. I could sure use the money. That job could help me pay room and board. I love kids, so I agreed to take on another part-time job.

It was easy to talk with Eric, but Jen intimidated me. She could be very direct. I told Eric I was afraid of Jen. He encouraged me to talk to her about it. Jen was surprised. As I opened up about how I felt the walls came down and we developed a wonderful friendship. Within a few months I landed a job working for a chiropractor as a chiropractic assistant. He trained me to do therapies on patients after they had their adjustment.

With my increased income Jen thought it would be good for me to get my own apartment. Just a two minute walk from her house was an apartment building which had studio apartments available for $175/month. I could afford that! I was told that the previous tenant had died in the apartment, and strange as it may seem, that didn't freak me out. I was able to buy his furniture from his family. Eric put a twin sized bed together for me and I moved in. Jen gave me some plates, a pot and some silverware to get me started. I had my own place—my very first apartment! The daydream I had in the Convent was coming true!

Living alone was hard at first. The apartment felt cold and empty. To avoid being alone I attended AA and Al-Anon meetings in the evenings. I also found a great women's AA meeting on Sunday afternoon which helped break up my weekend. As luck would have it I lived just blocks from AA Central Service where many meetings were held. I started making friends. I also started attending ACA—Adult Children of Alcoholics—Al-Anon meetings on Tuesday and Thursday evenings.

My counselor Sister Carol encouraged me to attend ACA to help me with my codependency issues. ACA was focused on recovering from the effects of growing up in an alcoholic family, especially with regard to relationship issues. It was the mid '80s and word was spreading as to the impact alcoholism had on families, not just the alcoholic. The ACA meetings were huge with anywhere from 40 to 100 people. I was given a copy of the ACA Laundry list when I went to an Al-Anon meeting while still in the Convent. I cried tears of relief as I identified with every single item on that list! There was a name for who I was—a 'diagnosis' and thus a 'cure'. If I attended these meetings and worked on my issues I could overcome these character defects. Some of the items on the ACA Laundry List included:

- We judge ourselves harshly and have a very low sense of self-esteem.
- We became isolated and afraid of people and authority figures.
- We became approval seekers and lost our identity in the process.
- We get guilt feelings when we stand up for ourselves instead of giving in to others.
- We either become alcoholics, marry them, or both, or find another compulsive personality such as a workaholic to fulfill our sick abandonment needs.
- We live life from the viewpoint of victims and are attracted by that weakness in our love and friendship relationships.
- We have an overdeveloped sense of responsibility and it is easier for us to be concerned with others rather than ourselves; this enables us not to look too closely at our own faults, etc.
- We become addicted to excitement.
- We confuse love and pity and tend to 'love' people we can 'pity' and 'rescue'.
- We have 'stuffed' our feelings from our traumatic childhoods and have lost the ability to feel or express our feelings because it hurts so much (denial).

Sister Carol was aware of this list and told me that there are positive aspects to being an ACA. For example, ACAs tend to be very compassionate and loyal. She said that each character defect could be changed to an asset—it was just a matter of finding balance.

I continued to see Sister Carol for my weekly counseling session. She helped me sort out my ACA issues. I didn't realize that I didn't know a lot of things. In ACA we'd say, "I didn't know that I didn't know." For example, I didn't know how to have fun sober. I realized that 'having fun' felt like a chore. I wasn't yet able to be spontaneous. I didn't know how to communicate honestly. I didn't know what I preferred or how to take care of myself in relationships. It was always about the other person, what they wanted or needed and whether they approved of me or not. It was never about what I wanted or needed—as if I'd know what my wants or needs were anyway. To speak up for myself felt IMPOSSIBLE and terrifying.

Sister Carol challenged me to start sharing at the ACA meeting—to raise my hand to speak, and tell the group, "I know I need to share, but I don't know what I want to say. My counselor told me I needed to raise my hand." As I told them how nervous I was I saw people nodding. They understood. Then I'd think of more to share. At first it was very anxiety provoking: my heart pounding, palms sweating—a real panic attack. But as I shared each week it gradually got easier. After the meeting people came up to me and told me they related to what I'd shared. That was amazing to me. I had always felt invisible, except when playing sports, and now people were seeing me and actually relating to ME!

After the meeting we'd go out for coffee and fellowship. One time a group of us went to see 'Rocky Horror Picture Show'. We had a blast watching the 'regulars', who were dressed up like the actors in the movie, get up on stage and act out the movie.

Though I was learning how to socialize and make friends in sobriety there were still times when I felt lonely. My feelings were thawing out from years of 'stuffing' them. Sister Carol taught me Separation Therapy. Separation Therapy is a technique where you separate out your Adult or Parent self from your Inner Child by listening for the emotion of the Inner Child. I saw my feelings as 'Little Kathy' and re-parented her by staying in my adult, or 'Big Kathy.' The Inner Child concept was gaining popularity with Rokelle Lerner, John Bradshaw and many others making huge contributions to the recovery field at that time. Sister Carol gave me a handout on this technique. I was journaling my feelings and getting more comfortable with this process.

One night while watching TV a sentimental commercial came on, like a family spending quality time together. I started crying. I thought "oh, this is a good time to try this out." So I said out loud, "Little, what's going on? Why are you crying?" I called Little Kathy

"Little" for short. Little said, aloud in a child's voice, "I miss my Mommy." I could feel her pain. She was sobbing. I flipped back to my Adult self and said, "I know you miss your Mommy. But she's 2000 miles away. I'm here, and I love you. I'll take good care of you." And I wrapped my arms around my tummy, giving Little Kathy a hug. Little relaxed and stopped crying. She felt reassured and loved. This sounds strange but the results were amazing. I'd do this kind of exercise when I could, either out loud or by journaling it out. Living alone had its benefits: I could cry when I needed to and I could pound pillows to release my anger without having to explain it to anyone. It was very convenient to have the freedom and the space to do this work.

During the first few years of my sobriety I had occasional drinking dreams. They felt so real. In the dream I'd be drinking a beer and all of a sudden realized I was supposed to be sober. I was so disappointed in myself. How could I let this happen? When I woke up I was so relieved. Yet I was afraid it could happen, so I'd be more vigilant not to relapse. I soon learned that this was normal in sobriety. It just confirmed that I truly was an alcoholic. Whenever I started wishing I had one last 'hurrah', one last party, I quickly reminded myself "I always have another drunk in me, but I may not have another chance at sobriety." This thought, along with not wanting to change my sobriety date nor disappoint God, kept me on target.

I continued to go to my meetings. The people in my Thursday night ACA meeting loved me into wholeness. They loved me when I felt unlovable. They saw something in me that I couldn't see yet—that I was precious and perfect as I was—a child of God. We were all getting healthy together. I found my first ACA Sponsor who, along with Sister Carol, showed me how to reparent myself. I had found Little and she was the heart and soul of me. Little was wounded but as I began to heal I discovered that Little was my source of wonder and love. From her came my zest for life. ACA recovery gave my heart and soul back to me, though I wouldn't have been able to do that work if I hadn't been sober. AA gave me my life back so I could then find my soul. Gradually I began to enjoy my own company, and became my own best friend. Living alone in my humble little apartment became a joy. The apartment was transformed from a cold room to a warm cocoon.

I continued to see Sister Mary Bernie once a month, updating her on how my recovery was progressing. She was very proud of me. I still wasn't sure what I wanted to do about Religious Life and she didn't push me. They were giving me a year to two years, so I had the time I needed to get to know myself in sobriety.

It was nice to see the Sisters. I came for dinner, stayed for the Divine Office and then met with Sister Mary Bernie. Usually, before I drove home, I would stop in at the large chapel for a quiet visit with God. It was a beautiful 'chapel in the round.' The peacefulness of that place enveloped me, like a warm embrace. As I sat there surrounded by the stained glass windows and the silence, I reflected on how busy my life had become with my job, AA and ACA meetings and building a social life. This was how my song 'Silence' came about:

Silence

There's a peace I find in Silence—Though I'm reluctant to
pass through its gate.
But when I do I find myself with You and the ecstasy was
worth the wait
The Love I find in Your Eyes lets me know I'm never alone
You're here with me—That's where I long to be
You've touched me and I have grown

Why do I run my day away—keeping too busy to hear what
You say
When all along I know whenever things go wrong
You're the One I turn to—to show me the way . . . .
And there's a Peace I find in Silence . . . .

Despite the fact that my life was going well, I longed for the safety and security of 'Home', of someone taking care of me, a safety net to catch me if I'd fall. Being a responsible adult, though invigorating at times, was also stressful. My parents had provided that safe haven for me, but now it didn't feel right to turn to them for help. I started noticing thoughts like, "If my car breaks down, I can always go back to the My Convent." My logic was rather distorted and my problem solving skills were anemic at best. Instead of seeking other solutions, I wanted to run back to the Convent, hoping the Sisters would take care of me, as they had in the past. I knew this was not responsible thinking. I was too embarrassed to admit this to anyone.

As I worked for the chiropractor it became apparent that he had a drinking problem. I saw him pop open a can of beer on the drive home as he pulled out of the parking lot. Also, he must have been drinking during lunch because when he returned he seemed extremely 'happy' for the rest of the afternoon. He ran late for his appointments, spending large amounts of time with patients when he was scheduled for only ten minute appointments. The office was chaotic as he usually ran up to an hour late. The patients were getting rather impatient as they waited to see the doctor.

I found myself preoccupied with his erratic behavior. I started to have 'blackouts' in sobriety. They call them codependent blackouts. A 'blackout' is when you are fully conscious but can't remember what occurred during a period of time. I'd forget if I'd done a therapy on a patient, check the therapy room only to see that the therapy had already been completed and they were gone. I was feeling incompetent in my job.

The Treatment Center I went through was right up the street, so I occasionally went there on my lunch break for a quick visit. One day I stopped by and told one of the counselors what was going on at work. She encouraged me to take part in their two week family program to address my codependency.

I told my boss that I was in recovery and needed two weeks off to address some issues. He graciously agreed. During the family program I learned more about codependency and how I was powerless over others. I was still unsure about my sexuality and wanted to use this as an opportunity to find some answers, but I was too nervous to bring it up. Then one day my counselor confronted me on how I dressed. "You dress like a tomboy." She was challenging me to grow up and be the young woman I was. Yet I was afraid to own my femininity. I was afraid that men would find me attractive. If they did, how should I respond? I still wasn't sure about the Convent and dating was not an option right now. Then she confronted me about using the Convent as an excuse to not grow up and be responsible. That's when I told her what I'd been thinking: "If the car breaks down I could always return to the Convent." I realized she was right. I decided that I must leave the Convent. Only then could I be free to choose what I wanted for my life, whether that meant returning to the Convent or something else.

I wasn't looking forward to my next meeting with Sister Mary Bernie. I nervously told her my decision. Though she was disappointed, she remained very supportive. I ended my leave of absence within a year of my departure. I left the Convent. I felt afraid, yet free. What did I want to do now? I still wasn't sure.

As I continued to work for the chiropractor, things got worse. I was still having trouble focusing on my job, preoccupied with the boss's behavior. Then one day he fired me. I couldn't believe it. It was like a bad dream. I thought I was a wonderful employee, but I didn't realize how much my job performance was suffering. I also wondered if my sober presence made my boss uncomfortable. Was it hitting too close to home?

Before I lost that job I met a patient named Jeanie who was also in recovery. I knew this when I saw the AA medallion on her key chain. I told her I was in recovery, too. Once I was fired she took me under her wing. She had her own house cleaning business and helped me get started with my own business. I had cleaned houses before entering the convent, so this was familiar to me.

Jeanie encouraged me to go back to college. Jen also thought returning to college to earn my degree was an excellent idea. "Once you have your degree no one can take it away from you," she told me. I qualified for Voc Rehab funding (due to my alcoholism) and decided to pursue a degree in Physical Education. It was fall of 1987. With my tuition paid, I started school, finishing my AA degree at the junior college, and went on to the university to complete my bachelor degree. I earned my B.S. in Education and graduated with honors in May of 1990. I cleaned my way through school, supporting myself with the $600 a month I made from my house cleaning jobs.

Jeanie was reunited with her high school sweetheart and moved out of state to be with him. She passed her house cleaning clients on to me. We eventually lost touch, but I am so grateful to Jeanie for her support and encouragement. I don't know if she realized what a difference she made in my life. I also owe a debt of gratitude to Eric and Jen. They were amazing. Eric was always available to help me when I had car trouble. Jen was like a big sister, showing me how to relate as an adult, sharing thoughts and feelings and accepting me where I was at the moment. Through it all I was always taken care of.

 **Reflection**

Separation Therapy proved to be invaluable in my journey to wholeness. Explore what will nurture your wholeness. It took many people to support my early recovery. Take time to reflect on your life and give thanks to those who nurture you along your way. Appreciate the challenges life offers. They are opportunities to expand and grow. Through the many changes, stay calm and know: You are always being taken care of.

Chapter 7

The Serenity Sisters

According to my Mom I was singing baby talk in the crib. I have always loved to sing. When I sing I feel peaceful and happy. As a child in the crib we sang "Mommy, I wanna get down," over and over again, until we got the desired result. I'm not sure who started that, me or Sue. We were quite the singing family. Dad loved to sing. He and his Mom had beautiful voices. As kids we made up songs to meet the situation. On our way to Grandma and Grandpa's house we sang, "We're almost there, we're almost there, we're almost there to Grandma and Grandpa's house." Then we sang it again, this time putting Grandpa first, giving him his just due. We loved spending time with them. Grandma was full of warm hugs and warm homemade chocolate chip cookies. Grandpa always had a trick or joke for us. He taught us how to sing the Schnitzelbank song, proudly showing us off to his neighbors. I'd always dreamed of being a singer.

The Serenity Prayer was the first time I ever took words and put them to music. I thought it was a fluke. "I'm not creative", I kept telling myself. But then one day my car broke down on the way home from one of my house cleaning jobs, providing an opportunity to write a song!

I had a new car, a 1987 Chevy Chevette—red, two door, 5 speed stick. I loved that car and called her 'Shatzi', after my Aunt Shatzi, my Godmother who I loved dearly. I didn't dare tell her that I named my car after her. I was afraid she would find it insulting, but they were both beautiful and special to me, just in different ways.

It was a cold, winter afternoon. I saw smoke coming from under the hood. I pulled over. As I opened the hood antifreeze was spilling all over the engine and onto the ground. I couldn't believe this happened to my new car. I had just let my AAA membership expire. Who needs that expense when I had a new car, right? I knew my engine would cook if I didn't get some antifreeze into it soon. I felt alone and scared. I wished I could call my Dad for help, only he was 2000 miles away. Then I thought of calling Eric, but then realized I knew what I needed to do.

"It's Ok," I tried to reassure Little and myself. "We just need to buy some coolant and get some water. I'll need just enough to make it to the car dealership." I saw an auto store about a mile away. I pulled myself together and started walking. The wind was whipping snow flurries around me. I gave Little a hug. "We're not alone. I'm here for you and God and Jesus are here for me," and I started to pray. "Help me get home safe. Please let it all work out."

I got to the store, bought engine coolant and asked for a jug of water. When I got back to my car I filled the radiator with a mix of coolant and water. I stopped one more time to fill the radiator before I got to the dealership. I only lived a couple of miles away so they kindly gave me a ride home.

That evening I was standing in my kitchen, looking out the window, washing dishes, and wondering if there would be a cost for the repair. I wasn't sure what was covered under my warranty. I started to get depressed thinking about the possible expense and how I was going to pay it. Realizing what I was doing, I told myself, "You need to stop this. Let's sing something uplifting." I started to play with the idea of smiling, and before I knew it, I was writing my song, 'Smile'. I stopped, went to my guitar and wrote out the words and chords. My first complete song, music and lyrics, was born.

Smile

Smile—Come on and Smile for Awhile
When the world looks gray—you've had a long day
You want to quit—You need to say
Smile
Come On and Smile for Awhile
The world looks bright and your load is light when you
Smile

Some days when nothing turns out right
It's all the strength I can muster not to get uptight
Just when I'm sure I've had enough
A little Voice inside says . . . . Smile . . .

Jesus said I'll never go it alone
But sometimes I feel I'm such a long way from home
He knocks at the door of my heart and says,
'Won't you let Me in, so we can . . . Smile'

You have a Power of your own
So open up and let the Power lead you home
You're the one who has to choose
The Strength is there for you in a . . . . Smile

I love school. Learning new things is fun to me. I missed playing sports while in the Convent. Majoring in physical education gave me an opportunity to take activity classes, i.e., swimming, basketball, soccer, etc. where we learned the skills for each sport and learned how to teach those skills to others. General education classes were also required for my degree. One of the classes I took was 'Teaching Exceptional Students'. It was a Special Education class on teaching students with disabilities. We were learning about mainstreaming, where those with disabilities were integrated into the regular classroom rather than segregated off to special schools. Mainstreaming was still in its infancy. There were many young adults with disabilities who had attended special schools prior to mainstreaming. I was given an assignment to interview such a person in order to better understand what their experience was like. At my ACA meeting I noticed a woman who was blind. Her name was Sue. I asked her if I could interview her for my class project. She agreed. That's how I got to know Sue, my singing partner for nine years.

Through our mutual recovery in AA and ACA, Sue and I became friends. We had known each other less than a year when we decided to drive over to Illinois for a Christmas celebration at Our Lady of the Snows. After dinner we drove through 'The Way of the Lights', which was the Christmas story with life-sized figures. There were sheep and shepherds, angels and the manger scene. As we drove we were serenaded with Christmas carols. I described the scene to Sue as I drove along. On the way home we started singing Christmas carols. I knew that Sue sang country music and had won the state's talent show a year or so ago. I wasn't much of a country music fan, but I was impressed by her award. As we started singing, Sue chimed in with harmony. It sounded so beautiful! "Let's see what she does with 'The Serenity Prayer'," I thought to myself. Obviously, Sue was familiar with the words in the chorus from AA and ACA meetings, but she'd never heard my song before. I started singing and Sue chimed in with this amazing harmony! We actually sounded very good together. I was blown away.

A few weeks later I was contacted by a woman I'd met at an AA retreat that I recently attended. While on the retreat I shared my Serenity Prayer song with the group and it was well received. She told me she was chairing a women's AA luncheon in a few months and asked if I'd like to share my song at the luncheon. I was freaked! I wanted to, but found the idea very intimidating. I told her I'd think about it. I asked Sue if she'd consider singing with me. We agreed to practice a few times to see how we sounded together.

It was amazing how our voices blended so beautifully, like we were meant to sing together! We sang about five songs, including 'Smile', at the luncheon, in front of an audience of five hundred women, and received a standing ovation. This was a dream come true though I was nervous as heck. After this event Sue and I got together for frequent practices as we began incorporating new songs into our act. I wrote new songs and Sue came up with amazing harmonies and echoes. We were a magnificent team.

Shortly after Sue and I started singing together I attended an Effective Living Seminar* at the Cenacle Sisters' Retreat house. It was a weekend of learning the power of our thoughts and how to visualize, in detail, what you desired to have in your life. The Seminar was similar to 'The Power of Positive Thinking' I'd read in 10th grade, only now it added the tool of visualization. Although I had begun to fulfill my childhood dream of sharing uplifting music with others, I was intensely nervous when performing. I hoped this Seminar would give me the tools necessary to overcome my self-consciousness.

They gave us a list of Six Necessary Basic Affirmations, beliefs which can empower one to manifest a happy, fulfilled life. I started saying them every day, repeating each one five times as instructed, saying them with conviction. At first they felt like a lie, but within a year I realized that, not only did I believe them, but they were coming true. Here they are:

1) I like myself unconditionally.
2) I never devalue myself through destructive self criticism.
3) I have unconditional warm regard for all persons at all times.
4) I am easily able to relax at any time, and every day through every affirmation I become healthier in mind, body and spirit.
5) I am completely self-determined and allow others the same right.
6) I am completely responsible for all my responses to all persons and to all events.

---

* The material from The Effective Living Seminar came from the work of John Boyle. He has since passed on and James Fadiman continues his work. The Six Basic Affirmations are used with permission to help spread the power of these affirmations. Please refer to Dr. Fadiman's book 'Unlimit Your Life: Getting and Setting Goals' for more information.

I added: I value myself through self acceptance and self-care.

I was also seeing a Sister of the Cenacle, Sister Pam, for spiritual direction. I'd meet with her once a month for about an hour. Spiritual direction provided a safe space to discuss my spiritual journey and my relationship with God. It was also an opportunity to connect my spiritual journey with the work I was doing in counseling and with my recovery from alcoholism and codependency.

I often struggled with how to cope with stress in a constructive way. When I felt overwhelmed I stopped doing those things that were healthy and nurturing. I laid down the very tools that would help me manage the stress, like meditation, AA meetings or calling my sponsor. Sister Pam told me, "It's like you're in a row boat on rough waters, and instead of using the oars to navigate yourself to safety, you throw them overboard." It was funny, but true. This image is an excellent reminder to hold on to my oars and put them to use.

I continued to struggle with feelings of inadequacy and shame. I wanted desperately to overcome these feelings that were holding me back from living my full potential. During one of our sessions Sister Pam asked if I was open to doing a guided imagery to explore the physical root of my shame. I was skeptical, but decided to give it a try. She asked me, "Where in your body do you feel the shame?" I checked in with my body and responded, "It's in my stomach, my gut." She asked me to describe what it looked like. I thought, "Oh, no. I'm not good at this. I won't see anything. You have to be able to let go and I'm just too controlling to do this. But I'll give it a try and see what happens." To my surprise I saw a brittle, dried up pine cone in my gut. Then the pine cone melted into a soft honeycomb filled with honey. I instinctively knew what this meant. I was changing from a rigid, scared child into a sweet, spontaneous, vibrant wonder child. My Inner Child was healing and I was becoming the sweet soul I was meant to be. I was so amazed and inspired by the positive changes happening in me that on the way home I wrote this song:

Honeycomb

I'm a Honeycomb—I'm a Honeycomb
Thank God, I'm a Honeycomb
No more fearful strife to taint my life
Thank God, I'm a Honeycomb—a Honeycomb

All those years of living in fear
Wouldn't let anybody draw near
Now your love and acceptance are setting me free
And I'm seeing the person I'm meant to be

I've longed for intimacy
Always wanted someone to love me
But it's always been safer to run and hide
And live like the pine cone I felt like inside

I feared the pine cone would stay
But now it is melting away
Into the softness, the sweetness and gentleness
Of the Real Child in Me who is Proud to Profess
I'm a Honeycomb . . . .

I felt somewhat uncomfortable sharing some of these songs with Sue, much less with our audience. Sometimes I needed to sit with a song for awhile before I was ready to share it. Sue was safe and affirming and that made it easier to share my music with her. As our song list increased, Sue and I shared them at 12 Step meetings whenever either of us was asked to speak. We called our talk 'Music in Recovery.' Some people didn't like my references to God/Higher Power as 'Lord', but that's where my spirituality was at the time. For the most part, we were well received.

We sang at an ACA retreat. Someone there put us in touch with his musician friends and they helped us record our songs. Sue and I did our best to scrape together the money we needed to finish our first project 'Serenity—Just for Today'. Our parents helped out by sending us money to support our project. We needed a group name. I remembered hearing the story of how the Doobie Brothers got their name. As I heard it told, they were usually hanging out together, making music and smoking 'doobies'. In case you don't know what a 'doobie' is, well, it's a marijuana cigarette. As I reflected on what Sue and I were about, these words started to come to me: recovery . . . serenity . . . spirituality . . . how about The Serenity Sisters?! We were Sisters in Recovery and our message was one of peace and spiritual growth.

Sue and I continued to sing at various 12-Step meetings: AA, ACA, OA—you name it. If we got asked to sing, we were there. We sang at Conventions and retreats. Then we decided we had a message for young people too. We began to offer our singing services to schools. This was during the Nancy Reagan years of 'Just Say No' to drugs. Our message was not only 'Just Say No' to drugs, but to 'Say Yes To Yourself and to Following Your Dreams'.

Our singing took us into prisons where we sang on REC (Residents Encounter Christ) weekend retreats and NA meetings once a month. We even appeared on KPBS at 2am New Years day a couple of times for their fundraiser. I remember trying to fix Sue's hair before we went on. "Kath, it's 2 o'clock in the morning. Who the heck is going to notice?" Sue said.

Many times Sue and I practiced in my little studio apartment. The Sutton bus loop was right outside. Sue heard the bus sitting outside my balcony and remarked, "There's our tour bus waiting to take us away!" I love Sue's wonderful sense of humor.

I continued to write songs. We eventually recorded three cassettes over a span of nine years. We later compiled the songs onto CD. We both dreamed of making it big someday sharing our music. I often wondered where God was leading us. I wrote 'Show Me the Way' as I reflected on my growth and uncertain future.

Show Me the Way

Lord, where do You want me to be
Where I can be Happy, Joyous and Free
Help me to let go and live for today
And help me to trust that You'll Show Me the Way

I've come so far from where I used to be
In learning just what it means to be me
But there's so much more yet that I long to do
And Lord, I want to give it all to You

Cuz You are a God so nurturing
You gave me the gift and desire to sing
Sometimes I wonder just what is Your plan
Oh, how I pray that some day I'll understand

And Lord, where do You want me to be
where I can be Happy, Joyous and Free
Help me to let go and live for today
And help me to trust that You'll show me the way

 # Reflection

We each have talents and gifts to share. What a natural high to give from your heart and to be of service by sharing your talents with others. Give yourself the gift of an open, loving heart by being of service to others. It will bring true happiness and satisfaction.

Chapter 8

To Thine Own Self Be True

I was still going to the women's Sunday AA meeting. It was wonderful how the women shared their feelings and experiences around sex and relationship issues and how they supported one another. I wanted to be able to raise my questions and share my concerns, but I feared their rejection. There were times I felt so alone that I had suicidal thoughts. I didn't want to kill myself, really. I wished it would all just go away. I longed for peace. I didn't want to lose my connection with God and feared that accepting my sexuality would cut me off from God. Most religions teach that Gay people, who express their sexuality, are condemned to Hell, right? But does God really discriminate based on our sexuality? God is Love—Unconditional Love. If we are loving in our relationships, how could God find this offensive? I continued to wrestle with these thoughts.

I was still seeing Sister Carol for counseling when I realized I needed to confess something. She was already aware of my attraction to women, but she didn't know everything. I was preoccupied with sexual fantasy. I found porn magazines in the bathroom of one of my house cleaning clients and lost control of my time by looking at them. I felt horrible about it, yet I couldn't stop. I decided I must let Sister Carol know what I was doing. I hadn't told a soul. I was so embarrassed and ashamed. On my way to my counseling appointment my car was acting funny, stalling out, but I was determined to get there.

By some miracle my car made it to the appointment, only to break down on the way home.

I told her what I'd been doing. She framed our discussion by reminding me that sexuality fell along a spectrum—Heterosexual . . . . Bisexual . . . Homosexual—and that we all fall somewhere along this range. I accepted that, but now I was into addictive behavior and needed help. I was beating myself up for my behavior and was sinking fast into my 'shit pit' of shame and despair. "What do I do? I'm afraid I can't keep away from it," I told her. She encouraged me to treat it just like alcohol—stay away from it all together—abstain. Since it was the secrecy and shame that were fueling my addiction to it, I was to call her for support, if I was tempted again. I knew that honesty and abstaining had worked with my addiction to alcohol, so I agreed. Just knowing that *she* knew and I was accountable to her kept me honest. I was able to stay away, however, the obsessive thoughts still hounded me.

Another year passed and I hadn't been able to resolve this issue, so I ended my therapy with Sister Carol and tried group therapy. When that proved ineffective I eventually entered counseling with Joan, a therapist who came highly recommended by a close friend. It was early September when I began dating a wonderful guy named Mark. He was everything I wanted in a man. He was kind and gentle, spiritual and sensitive, handsome and in recovery, and best of all, he was a terrific kisser! Yet after awhile I still found myself drawn toward women. Well, actually the feeling of attraction never left. I was just so happy to be what I thought was 'in love' with a man and he with me. I felt relieved to be 'normal'. But once the infatuation died down, there it was again. I felt jealous that men got to be with women. I knew I needed to do something. I decided to go to 12 Step meetings for sex addicts. My obsessive thoughts felt like an addiction. Maybe the meetings would help. I met wonderful people there and made some good women friends. I was able to talk about my struggles and they didn't run screaming from the room. The shame dissipated. I told Mark about it and he was very supportive, though he questioned my calling it an addiction. Recently my good friend George pointed out, "It's interesting that you could identify yourself as a sex addict but you couldn't identify yourself as being Gay." I guess my longing for a solution that met with others' approval was just **that** strong. I was willing to go to any lengths to flip the switch and be 'Straight'.

Joan had an amazing ability to listen deeply and was able to see the dynamics of my approach to life within the very first session. She told me, "You have a tendency to label things—to put things in nice, neat compartments—in order for life to make sense to you. Although this can be helpful at times, it sounds like you do it to such a degree that you're blocking your spontaneity. Life is rarely that neat and tidy." She continued, "I can see that we may butt heads as I challenge you to view life from different perspectives." Her statements shook me to the core. I wanted to be an 'A' student, even in therapy, and longed for her approval. I had a feeling I was in for quite a ride.

After working with Joan for several months, discussing my attraction to women and my addiction to sexual fantasy, Joan asked me, "Kathy, just what is your addiction?" I had to think about that for a minute. Then I knew. "I'm addicted to not being responsible," I told her. It was then that I realized I needed to date women responsibly in order to determine my sexual orientation. Was I Bi or Gay? I needed to know. I needed peace. I learned in AA that God's will for us is to be 'Happy, Joyous and Free'. I also learned in the Convent that peace was a sign of the Holy Spirit. I had been dealing with this issue throughout my four years of sobriety. I was so tired of the struggle that I was ready to take the risk.

In order to Come Out I needed to let Mark know right away what I had decided. We had plans to get together to see Amy Grant in concert at the Fox on December 8th, 1988. We went to dinner beforehand. That's when I told him, "Mark, you know I love you. And you know I've been struggling with my attraction to women. Well, I think I may be Gay, or at least Bi. I have to date women to find out." Mark was relieved. We hadn't been as sexual as he would have liked. "Good for you, Kath. You need to date women and find out. And I need to date other women, too." We both laughed. We'd become great friends during our few months of dating and I knew we'd continue to be friends. We enjoyed Amy's concert knowing that we wouldn't see each other for awhile. We both needed time apart in order to move on with our lives.

Joan gave me a book to read, 'Beyond Acceptance', written by parents in P-Flag. P-Flag is a support group for parents, family and friends of Lesbians and Gays. I'd never been to a meeting but Joan told me the groups were very supportive and accepting. I eventually attended the group meetings and found them very helpful. I received acceptance, love and support from the parents in the group. I wondered if I'd ever experience that from my own parents.

I was preparing for my trip to New York to see my family over Christmas. I took the book home with me, kept it safely out of sight in my room, and read it in the evenings. By the time I got back to St. Louis Joan noticed how I seemed more comfortable with being Gay. I was looking forward to the New Year when I'd venture out and explore the Gay community.

Some people Come Out by going to Gay bars. Others take out a personal ad. I decided to attend a Lesbian AA meeting. I figured it was the safest way to Come Out. I met a whole new group of people. I started to feel like a part of the group. I also ran into a young woman I knew from the Treatment Center who I knew was Gay, though she had known me as Straight. "Since when are you Gay?" she asked. "All my life, I guess. I'm only now accepting it," I replied. I felt freer than I'd ever felt before, other than when I got sober. I didn't like the term 'Lesbian'. It sounded too strong, too 'in your face'. I was more ok with 'Gay'. As I got more honest with myself, I accepted that I was 'Gay', not 'Bi'. 'Bi' for me just wasn't true. Though I believe some people truly are Bi, for me it was another form of denial.

As I reflected on my dating history with men I realized a few things. When I thought I was in love it was partly because I liked being liked

AND I wished I was him. He got to be with women. I always wished I could. Now I was able to, but who? Then I met a beautiful woman at my AA meeting. She had dark hair, dark eyes, a beautiful face and warm smile. We talked a few times after the meeting. Then I invited her to a basketball game at the local college.

Date night arrived and I was SO nervous. I was 25 years old and on my first REAL date. But, was this really a date? It was a date to me, but how did she see it? I was so confused! At the basketball game, we talked a lot as we watched the women's game. I explained what was happening with each play. She wasn't that familiar with basketball. Teaching her about the game gave us something to talk about. It also gave me a reason to look at her beautiful face. Then the men's game started and we ran out of things to say. I was so nervous. We went for coffee after the game. I told her about my singing. She told me she had a guitar. When I brought her home I came in to see her guitar and to sing a couple of songs for her. When we hugged good night I asked if I could kiss her. She said 'yes.' We kissed. How heavenly! "How could I have missed out on this for so long? She's so soft, so wonderful!" We held each other for awhile longer, and then I left.

We went out a few more times. I was grateful to God for bringing her into my life. I thought I had found 'The One', but within a few weeks of dating she told me she wasn't ready for a relationship. She had just ended a relationship a few weeks before. She needed time to heal. At first I was crushed, but then I thought that if I could be patient and hang around I'd make her fall in love with me. That never happened. I eventually realized that our personalities didn't really click. I had been caught up in physical attraction. This was all new to me—to feel attracted to someone and be able to express it. My life had just opened up in a totally new way!

As I let go of shame over my feelings and was true to myself, I noticed the obsessive sexual thoughts disappeared. Joan had taught me that when a feeling is denied, it gets distorted. Anger, for example, when denied can lead to rage or depression. Now that I was accepting myself I felt energized and free. My energy wasn't being wasted on guilt and shame. My creativity took off. And I was finally growing up—taking responsibility for all aspects of my life.

 ## Reflection

The greatest act of self love is being true to yourself. Yet you can't be true to yourself until you know who you really are. We are each beautiful, powerful Lovers and Creators. We were created that way—in the Image and Likeness of God.

Accept yourself, thrive and be happy!

Chapter 9

Finding My Spiritual Home

I started going to Dignity on Sunday evenings. Dignity is an organization for Catholic Gay people who want to celebrate the Mass and practice their faith and not have to be closeted. I went a few times, and met some very nice people. However, it bothered me that we had to celebrate on Sunday evening, not Sunday morning, and that we were the 'outcasts' of the Catholic Church. I felt like I was still trying to win Mom and Dad's approval and I was tired of it.

My first best Gay friend was a woman I met in AA named Michelle. She was a sweet, happy soul. She kept telling me about all the wonderful people at her Church. Michelle's Church was MCC of Greater St. Louis, which stands for Metropolitan Community Church. MCC is a Christian Church founded in the late 1960s to minister to the Gay, Lesbian, Bisexual and Transgendered Community (LGBT). The Church was putting on a variety show and Michelle asked if Sue and I wanted to perform. Sue was open to it. Sue had been very supportive of my coming out. She was sensitive to discrimination due to her own experiences as a blind person. We sang a couple songs and they loved us. We were so excited! Then I sang my song called 'Is It Ok?' which is a prayer I wrote during my Coming Out process. The crowd really loved it! Below are the words I'd like to share with you.

Is It Ok?

Is it ok to be Gay
Oh, Lord, what do you say?
I've fought this one for such a long time
Tried to deny these feelings inside
Now I know I need to be
Just who I am so I can be free

Rules thrown around in Your name
Telling me how to play their game
Are devoid of Your love and Your tender Mercy
Are as tight as a straight jacket tied around me
Have left me all but dead inside
Longing for You to be by my side

I need to love and be loved
For this is a gift given from Above
Does it matter to You which sex I choose
Even if other's acceptance I lose
Serenity is Your answer to me
Thank you for loving and setting me free

Yes, It's Ok to be Gay
Oh, Lord, I'm hearing You say
"My commandment to you is to love tenderly
Be true to yourself, don't act selfishly
To honor, respect and to live gently
With yourself, with others and Me"

After such a warm welcome I became curious about their Church, so I started to attend their service on Sunday mornings. I really enjoyed it. The people were so loving and accepting. I felt right at home. The service was similar enough to the Catholic Mass yet different enough that I felt free to be myself. I was happy that they celebrated communion each week, that they had the readings from the Old and New Testament and a homily by the pastor. The music was fun and inspirational, and, unlike my experience in the Catholic Church, everybody sang.

I eventually joined the choir and sang special music every couple of months. After I attended for awhile I decided to become a member. This was a Protestant Church. I felt SO guilty as I walked up to the altar with a few other people to make our profession of faith and commitment to this spiritual family. The old tapes began to play, "You're leaving the Catholic Church. How dare you! Once a Catholic, always a Catholic. How could you leave the One True Religion?" I observed my thoughts and reassured myself, "It's Ok. After all you've been told through the years, it's natural to feel guilty. But you're doing the right thing." I reminded myself that peace is a sign of the Holy Spirit. I knew in my heart that this path was life giving. I felt loved and accepted by God. I was no longer concerned about the Catholic teachings.

Leaving the Catholic Church wasn't as hard as Coming Out, but it was still difficult. I reminded myself repeatedly to let go of the guilt. I was on a new path, and it felt great. I liked what Pastor Brad said during the ceremony, "We give thanks for every spiritual family who has nurtured you along the way." Yes, I was grateful for many things the Catholic faith gave me. But I didn't need to hand my power over to the Pope, Bishops and priests who didn't even know me nor understand me. These people would no longer define what was right for me. I was taking responsibility for my faith and for my life. Once again, I claimed my spiritual path as my own.

At one point our Church began to have prayer partners who were available to pray with people after communion. I had gotten used to praying aloud while in the convent. Though it felt awkward at first, I discovered that I enjoyed ministering to others through prayer. I signed up to be a prayer partner. It was a very powerful experience to be used as an instrument of healing, praying for someone's intention. I felt God's power and peace as I held hands with the person I was praying with.

I grew spiritually and felt more confident by being a part of MCC. I developed meaningful relationships there with adopted sisters, brothers, Moms and Dads. They were my spiritual family. These people knew my darkest secret and loved me because they too had shared that secret and had learned to love and accept themselves. One thing that still bothered me was that I hadn't Come Out to my parents. Occasionally they would ask if I was dating anyone. I hated lying to them, but I didn't dare tell them about my self-discovery and that I was dating women. I had told some of my brothers and sisters and they were all very supportive. But when it came to my parents, it would be hard to break the news. I debated how to tell them—in person, in a letter, or over the phone? I spoke with my friends at Church and to the parents at P-Flag to get some encouragement. They all had different experiences and told me it was my decision as to how to Come Out to my parents. I was Out three years when I decided that telling them in person was the best choice for me. I didn't want any misunderstanding and wanted to be able to reassure them that God was OK with this and that I was happy.

The time had arrived. I was home for my brother's wedding. I planned to tell them the next day. I had so much fun dancing with my sisters at the wedding reception. I hoped my parents noticed and would see how happy I was. I gave my Siblings a 'heads up' and they cleared the house to avoid the explosion we all knew was imminent. My plan was to tell them, discuss it for a while, and then leave the house so they could have time to digest the news.

I was nervous. When the words came out of my mouth, "Mom and Dad, I'm Gay", I could see how far apart we'd grown. Mom said, "Please tell me you're joking." Dad was silent for what felt like an eternity. Then he laid into me. "What do you mean, you're Gay? What happened to you out there in St. Louis? Who did this to you? I can't believe this. How could you do this? After all we taught you." I tried to explain how difficult it had been for me to accept myself. I told them that God was OK with this, and that I knew it would take time for them to digest this information. I wanted them to know that I was still the same person; that I was happy and at peace. They couldn't hear it. They were hurt and disappointed, to say the least. Dad didn't even say goodbye to me when I left for the airport the next day. We've always loved each other, but they had no frame of reference for this. The only thing they knew about being Gay was what the Catholic Church had taught them about homosexuality. The teaching was that if you happen to be Gay, you must choose celibacy. In the eyes of the Church, to act on it was a perversion of God's gift of sexuality. My heart ached knowing that I had caused them so much pain—just by being true to myself.

I didn't see my parents for quite some time. When we talked on the phone they'd eventually bring up the issue, asking if I had come back to God and the Catholic Church. Several times I told Dad I needed to hang up if he continued to lecture me, and a few times I did. At one point I was afraid he'd drive out from New York to kidnap me and take me to some 'make-em Straight' camp. It took three years before we reached an agreement. I called them while taking a self growth seminar. I told them I loved them and missed them very much. I was planning to drive home in a few months for a visit and would love to see them. Dad told me he loved me too and that he'd love to see me. Mom agreed. Though she was disappointed about my being Gay, Mom was always pushing for a peaceful resolution. I think most Moms are like that. We all agreed to disagree, choosing love over right or wrong. We dealt with it by just not talk about it. It wasn't the best scenario, but somehow it worked.

The first time I saw them since Coming Out was when they visited our camp site. I was camping with Sue, my singing partner, and my friend, Susan. We were making a fire and cleaning up after dinner. Dad walked right up to me and gave me a huge hug. It felt wonderful to be embraced by his strong arms. As we sat around the camp fire that evening, Sue and I serenaded them with our music. Though we never discussed the 'Gay' thing, it was nice having my parents back in my life.

 **Reflection**

We all have the right to find our own spiritual path—a Haven that nurtures our spiritual growth and where we can find true connection with God / Spirit.

Chapter 10

Relationships—Even Gay Ones—Aren't Easy

I thought Coming Out would solve my relationship issues. How naïve of me! I quickly discovered that I brought my issues with me. My first relationship lasted only 3 months. My longest relationship in those first five years lasted about a year and a half. I repeated the same old pattern. Let's call it Pattern A: Someone liked me. I felt great to be noticed. Then I got caught up in being liked and confused THAT with being in love. Coming Out at the age of 25, I guess I was a little impatient in choosing a partner.

It took me awhile to know how I really felt about the other person. Dating is supposed to provide the opportunity to get to know someone before committing, but I'd get involved too quickly and not notice the red flags telling me this wasn't a good fit. I felt like a rotten person for breaking it off and hurting their feelings. Breaking up went against all my peace-maker instincts. Though I wasn't in love, I did get to know some truly wonderful people.

I wrote this song after the break-up of my first relationship. It reflects my confusion, heart-ache as well as my belief about finding 'the right one'.

Love's Door

I went too fast—All I wanted was a love that would last
You needed me so—I didn't realize I could have said 'No'
Cuz I needed you too—and to hear the words 'I do love you'
But there's got to be more—than being fearful to walk through
Love's Door

Chorus:
And what is Love anyway—won't you please tell me
I'm so unsure—what lies beyond Love's Door

I wanted romance—the chance to do things I'd never done
Now here I am—wishing I had waited for the right one
When you came along—I was so blinded on my need
My need to be loved—that in us I needed to believe

Then there was Pattern B: I was in love but chose people who needed fixing, so I became their hero. I enjoyed being needed and 'special' in their eyes. These chaotic relationships robbed me of serenity as I learned the hard way that I could not change another person. Luckily, I didn't relapse over relationship issues.

It was tough Coming Out as an adult, and having to deal with the emotions and hormones that most Straight people experience and begin to work through as teenagers. Relationships can be messy, and I felt embarrassed as I experienced such messiness in my life.

While going through one painful break up I wrote the following song:

Peeling the Onion

Peeling another layer off the onion
Going another level deep
The pain hurts so much
Still I'm glad that I'm in touch
And Progress is mine to keep

Saying goodbye is never easy
Still there comes a time for letting go
It's not working anymore
And God knows what's in store
When you get down the road a piece you'll see

That to Live is to Change
When it's time to rearrange you'll know
God will give you the strength
You've got what it takes to grow
So, Trust the Process and Let Go
Trust the Process and Let Go

Peeling another layer off your onion
Pain so intense you want to die
Grab some Courage and hold tight
God will see you through the night
With the Strength to give it one more try

And to Live is to Change

Some say that life is a school. If so, relationships are the core part of the curriculum. We never graduate and earn a degree, no matter how fast we learn. I once heard at an ACA meeting: "Relationships are like putting Miracle Grow on your character defects." Want to know what your issues are? Get into a relationship! Relationships tend to expose our vulnerabilities and our insecurities. At times we tend to act from our neediest self. But therein lays the opportunity to grow and heal, if we and our partner are willing to do the work.

Here are a few relationship lessons I learned in therapy. The first valuable lesson was about communication. I remember Joan told me in one of my therapy sessions, "When in doubt, communicate." Anytime I had an issue with someone and I didn't know what to do about it, I could hear Joan reminding me to talk it out. There's a tendency to act based on our assumptions, and we all know what happens when we assume . . .

The second lesson I learned during this time was: "Ask for what you need and accept what you get." Once you communicate your needs honestly, directly and lovingly, you have no control over how the other person will respond. It's important to remember this or you may end up very disappointed or frustrated. Even if your request is denied, at least you have let the other person know where you stand. In Al-Anon I also learned, "Don't go to the hardware store to get a loaf of bread," meaning, when you need something specific, go to the person who can give that to you. To request or even demand something of someone that they are either unwilling or unable to give is self defeating and unfair, both to you and the other person.

That's all I have to say about relationships. I'm still a novice in this area. I thank those in my past for their love and for the opportunity to learn and grow. I wish them nothing but the very best!

After one break-up I lamented to my sponsor how I wish I would have listened to my gut. My sponsor suggested that I channel my disappointment into a song. I am not usually able to write songs on cue, but this one came to me rather easily.

Listen to Your Gut

Listen to your gut when it tells you what's up
Cuz you know it's right . . . most of the time
That Little Voice well it's got no choice
But to tell you what's going on

My troubles are of my own making
Cuz I want what I want right now
My life is a mess, but you'd never guess, that I just don't know how
How to Listen to my gut . . . .

80

Relationships aren't easy—and we all want love in our life
But it's better to wait—it's never too late
When it don't feel right
You got to Listen to your gut . . . .

It's taken so much time, mmm, but now I've come to find
The answers I've been searching for are right here inside
Got to Listen to your gut . . . .

 **Reflection**

Relationships offer us opportunities to learn and to grow. Remind yourself that it's OK to make mistakes, and when you do, forgive yourself. Remember: No one is perfect.

Be patient and loving with yourself and ask: "What can I learn from this?" and "What have I learned about myself?" If you can, keep a journal to see your patterns and mark your progress. Below are valuable lessons I learned over the years:

1. Be true to yourself.
2. Relationships require give and take. Are you constantly giving . . . or taking?
3. Like attracts like. Get healthier and you will attract a healthier mate.
4. Forgive—yourself and others.
5. Take responsibility for your thoughts, words and actions.

Chapter 11

'Go West, Young Woman'

Pay attention to those things you're drawn to—those tugs—those things that fascinate you—that grab your attention. I heard John Bradshaw and Wayne Dyer both mention this, and I've found it to be true. At one time while living in St. Louis I was fascinated about California, even considered moving there, but I didn't follow through on it. I fell in love and got distracted by a relationship. Another time Arizona caught my attention, but I put that off due to another relationship. Luckily the Arizona 'tug' didn't go away.

At the time I was having issues in my relationship. It had been a difficult one—Pattern B. My Pastor at MCC and his partner announced they were moving to Phoenix, Arizona to lead the Church there. I'd been seriously considering a move to Phoenix and then this happened! I saw it as confirmation that I should make the move. With my Pastor close by, it would make the move a little bit easier. I checked with my employer and they had an office in Phoenix. There was a job opening I qualified for. I flew out for an interview and landed the job!

If it sounds like everything went smoothly, well, that's only half true. I had reservations about leaving St. Louis. First, I'd be leaving Sue and the Serenity Sisters. We had been singing together for nine years. Sue's friendship and our music had been a huge part of my life. Although I loved singing with Sue and sharing our message, I felt drawn to minister in other ways, beyond what our music could offer.

I wanted to become a counselor and empower others to become whole. I'd thought long and hard about getting an MSW (Master of Social Work) at Arizona State University. It was affordable and seemed like a good fit for me as it was marketable and versatile. The only MSW program in St. Louis at that time was at St. Louis University, which is a private school and very expensive.

Secondly, I'd be leaving my relationship. We were together for about a year. We had decided to break-up, only to get back together. Throughout that year we'd had our share of ups and downs. I loved her—let's call her Mary—and felt she was the 'One'.

From the beginning there were red flags. She had a tendency to allow others to take advantage of her good nature and this led to financial disaster. She smoked and smelled like an ashtray. She didn't smoke around me at first and promised she'd quit. That never happened. Looking back, I don't know how I got past that, but sometimes love is blind. She didn't drink alcohol that often but when she did she usually got drunk and would sometimes black out (a sign of alcoholism). At first I denied what I was seeing, minimizing it. After all, she didn't drink that frequently, but as we continued to have problems, my denial started to wear down. I began to see things more clearly. I confronted her but she denied there was an issue. Then one day it struck me: I didn't go through the painful process of getting sober to end up in a relationship with an active alcoholic.

On the other hand, she was beautiful and fun to be with. Our chemistry was amazing. Deep down I knew the relationship wasn't healthy for me, but I was hooked. I was her rescuer—her hero. Each time I stepped in to save the day she'd tell me I was her saving angel and it stroked my ego. My codependency was in full swing. I was on a roller coaster ride with her chaotic life, and I knew I needed to get off.

After a year we broke up. It was mutual at first, but then she made it sound like I broke up with her. It was hard to stand my ground and not get back together. We eventually did reconcile, but not before I decided to move to Phoenix to pursue my degree at ASU.

Mary didn't want me to leave. We agreed to stay in touch and see where our relationship went. I hoped that she would eventually get honest with herself about her issues. Maybe the time apart would help us both. She helped me drive out to Phoenix. Once we hit Arizona, we took time to drive up to the Grand Canyon. It was like the honeymoon we never had. Upon our arrival in Phoenix, reality set in. She would be leaving in a few days. I felt bad about leaving her. It was incredibly hard to say goodbye.

I slowly got settled into my apartment and my new job. I missed Mary immensely and thought I'd made a mistake. We talked frequently on the phone, crying about how much we missed each other. Then one Sunday at Church I went to a prayer partner after communion. She prayed with me and I began to cry. She seemed to know my situation. "You needed to leave. You're in the right place. God brought you here to speak to your heart and to get you back on track." I felt reassured. As we became friends, I learned that she had psychic abilities. She helped me see that Phoenix was a temporary stop on my way to California, and that San Diego was where I'd ultimately end up. I've always been open to psychics. I know there are frauds out there, but I believe some people really have a gift. I was excited to have this sense of direction.

While in Phoenix I also reconnected with my friend Clare. I'd known Clare since 'Convent Land', when she was a nun in a different community. We met in Aftercare after I completed the very first family program, and before I went into treatment for alcoholism. We lost touch after I left the Convent. Then we bumped into each other at an ACA meeting. It turned out she had left the Convent as well. She had moved to Phoenix about eight years before me.

Clare was very supportive and helped me through a rough time after my break-up with Mary. Clare quoted from the Bible, "I will draw her to the desert and there I will speak to her heart." She told me that God led me to Phoenix so I could reconnect with Him. Being here would help me re-focus on my spiritual path.

I was in Phoenix for two and a half years. I never did get my MSW. It didn't seem like the right time for school. I needed time to heal and grow. A few times a week before work I'd hike to the top of Squaw Peak, growing strong physically and spiritually. 'Slow and Steady—One Step at a Time' was my hiking mantra.

I continued to attend MCC Gentle Shepherd in Phoenix, where I sang and was a prayer partner. I made some wonderful friends. My codependency was in check and I got back in touch with my path. I read the 'Conversations with God' series which opened my mind and expanded my beliefs. In those books Neale Donald Walsh converses with God via automatic writing. The concepts shared in the book offers a much broader perspective on life than what traditional Christianity teaches. I appreciated this newer perspective.

While in St. Louis I'd read Marianne Williamson's book 'A Return to Love', in which she reflects on the principles of 'A Course In Miracles' (ACIM). I loved how Marianne explained The Course. I wanted to learn more, so I bought a copy of ACIM and began to read it while I was in Phoenix. I couldn't understand it. It kept mentioning 'The Son of God', which I understood as Jesus. I have since learned that 'Son of God' refers to all of us. Even though I didn't comprehend its message, I was amazed by how peaceful I felt while reading it. I'd heard that the Course was channeled from Jesus to a woman in the 1970's. I love Jesus and wanted to hear directly from Him. I knew that the Bible had been translated and interpreted in so many ways that I didn't always trust its message. To hear directly from Jesus—now, THAT was worth listening to! Yet I found the Course confusing. I made a mental note to get back to ACIM at some point, hoping that somehow, some way, I would come understand Jesus' message.

I continued to go home to New York in the summer to see my family. My parents had retired and moved to Florida. They spent the summer in New York, so I was able to see them along with the rest of my family. After one of my visits I was so troubled by my Dad's drinking and the condition of his health that I felt compelled to talk with him about it. I kept getting an image of a pickle. It starts as a fresh cucumber, but once pickled it is changed forever. Grandma used to make pickles from the cucumbers in her garden, so this process was very real to me. It seemed Dad had pickled himself with alcohol. I was worried about his health, and nervous about bringing this up with him. After talking my concerns over with my sponsor, who was a drug and alcohol counselor, I felt I needed to say something. I called him up one day. I told him I loved him and that I was worried about his health due to his drinking. He acknowledged that he was concerned about his drinking too. He said, "I know I have my weaknesses and I'm asking God for help." I tried to assure him that it was an illness and there was a way out. I told him I was praying for him. He continued to drink for another few years.

At first being in Phoenix felt like a vacation—palm trees—sunshine—warm weather. I was in Phoenix about a year when the heat finally got to me. The temperature hit 118 degrees! I walked out of work one day, from the cool air conditioned building, and felt like my brain was about to boil. 'A dry heat' . . . . yes, but still, 118 degrees is #@$%# HOT! It was as if I was standing next to a bar-b-que pit. I couldn't take the heat and needed to get 'out of the kitchen'! A friend in AA was moving to San Diego and asked if I'd help by driving the U-Haul. While in San Diego for the weekend move we went to a Halloween dance. I met someone there and we dated long distance for a year. I had hoped to move to San Diego eventually and this seemed like the perfect opportunity. I was able to land a job and moved to San Diego within a year of meeting her.

While in San Diego I went to school to become a drug and alcohol counselor. I also received training in grief counseling. I loved the classes and looked forward to using my training to empower others.

During this time my Dad passed away. He had stopped drinking about a year before his death, saying "I just don't have an appetite for it anymore." Even his appetite for food suffered, though he still enjoyed eating his beloved sandwich. Dad developed an abdominal aneurism and needed surgery. All of his kids called the week before the surgery to wish him well, to tell him we were praying for him and that we loved him. In the back of my mind I knew I needed to say some things 'just in case.' I told him I loved him and thanked him for being *my* Dad. We reminisced about the good times we'd had together: sitting on his shoulders in the pool as he 'back flipped' us into the water, the numerous hiking and camping adventures, playing Santa for us, digging ditches for one project or another, and gathering wood for winter to feed the wood burning stove. He was a wonderful Dad.

Unfortunately, Dad never woke up from the surgery. His liver was severely damaged and they couldn't stop the bleeding. He passed away peacefully. We were all in a state of shock. This wasn't supposed to happen. He was only 65 years old. He'd been on blood pressure and strong heart medications for many years, but we knew his drinking also played a role. I put my newly acquired grief training into practice by encouraging my siblings to make collages and write their memories of Dad to share at his memorial service. It helped move us through the grieving process.

I took a break from church for awhile. I'd gotten deeper into meditation. I loved the silence and the peace of meditation. I took a series of meditation classes and learned to focus my mind and became aware of the 'Silent Observer'—the Higher Self. I felt surges of peace pulsating through my body as I meditated, focusing on my breath, and then on the dark screen before me—the quiet, empty mind. Meditation provided a natural high. I longed to experience it often, so I made time to meditate daily for at least twenty minutes or more. When I went to my AA meetings I wanted to identify myself this way: My name is Kathy and I'm a meditator' rather than saying 'I'm an alcoholic.'

I visited Self Realization fellowship, founded by Paramahansa Yogananda. I read his book, 'The Autobiography of a Yogi' and was intrigued by the Saints of India. As a former Catholic, I found it refreshing to see that God's miraculous power was not restricted to Catholicism nor Christianity. I realize now how close minded that sounds! I loved Paramahansa Yogananda's teachings, especially about detaching from material things and wanting God, only God, making God the center of one's life. I attended Self Realization

Fellowship a few times and loved the peaceful power of group meditation. I also attended Unity and enjoyed the positive message there, especially the use of affirmations. I was intrigued by their study of 'A Course In Miracles', though I never attended any of their classes.

 **Reflection**

Make time for meditation. It will increase your concentration, your serenity and your insight. Pay attention to those 'tugs'—those 'fascinations'—that come to you. You may not know what they mean or where they'll lead you, but looking back you may find a hidden treasure was discovered by following them.

Chapter 12

Further Spiritual Expansion

I worked as a drug and alcohol counselor for a short time. I really enjoyed the work though it could be heart breaking to see patients relapse and not make it back. While working at a treatment center one of the counselors introduced me to Louise L. Hay's book and CD called 'I Can Do It'. It was a good reminder of the power of affirmations. I used Louise's CD with the patients in treatment. In her book Louise mentioned a teacher named Abraham. I checked out Abraham-Hicks.com and found a wealth of empowering information. It reinforced what I already knew: that our thoughts have the power to create our life experience. I was reminded that we are spiritual beings, a part of Source Energy—God. Abraham reminds us that we live in a vibrational universe. Everything is vibrational—not only the sounds we hear, but what we see, taste and touch—even our thoughts—carry a vibration. I learned that my emotions reflect the thoughts I've been thinking. They indicate where I am vibrationally. Abraham calls our feelings 'the emotional guidance system.' This bit of wisdom has served me well as I let my emotions give me feedback and guide me to better feeling thoughts and higher vibrations. As Abraham says, 'Good feels good.' It's that simple. You can't create good things in your life from a place of negativity.

The Law of Attraction basically means that 'Like attracts like'—and confirms that 'what goes around, comes around'. So, for example, if I am loving and think and act from love, loving people and situations will show up in my life. If I'm feeling down and depressed it's because

I'm either thinking depressing thoughts or seeing the events in my life in a depressing way. An optimistic perspective, i.e., seeing the glass half full, will serve you much better than a pessimistic perspective, seeing the glass half empty. Abraham taught me how to purposely move up the emotional scale, from feeling down and depressed to feeling happy and appreciative. By doing so One Step at a Time, just like I learned in AA, I learned to guide my thoughts toward feelings of relief and a happier place.

At first I thought it was 'bad' to have negative feelings. But after listening to Abraham's interactions with others (via CD, DVD and by attending a workshop), I heard them say "make peace with where you are and then reach for feelings of relief." I had learned from my recovery not to deny my feelings, but sometimes I'd wallow in self pity, fear or regret. This only made matters worse and delayed the healing process. It has been immensely helpful to practice Abraham's guidelines for how to work with my emotions.

I loved the work of Abraham-Hicks and found Louise L. Hay's work to be along the same philosophy, so I went through training to become a Heal Your Life workshop leader and coach. I was just beginning that work when I landed a job as a health coach. I really enjoy working with people to empower them to 'believe in themselves and follow their dreams.' Counseling has its place, for sure, but I love the empowering nature of coaching: present moment, solution focused, looking forward to creating the future you desire.

Around this time I began to question who Jesus really was. Traditional Christianity teaches that Jesus is the Son of God, a part of the Blessed Trinity—Father, Son and Holy Spirit. I began to question, "Then who are we? Aren't we the children of God? I believe we are. So how can Jesus be 'The Only Begotten Son of God' when we're also God's children?" The traditional Christian teachings didn't make sense to me anymore. I began to see Jesus as an Evolved Soul, a Master Teacher, an Older and Wiser Brother, who was sent to show us the way Home. With this new realization I just couldn't go back to traditional religion. This all culminated one Christmas Eve when I found myself taking a walk in the cool December air. I decided to go to a Christmas Eve service, wanting to celebrate Christmas 'like the old days', but on this walk I found myself sobbing. I was grieving the loss of Jesus, my Divine Savior. The old familiar Christmas Carols had lost their meaning. I felt homesick for the Jesus I once knew. I was undergoing a transformation which was opening me up for more. But in the mean time I felt estranged from my Buddy Jesus.

Shortly after finding Abraham and losing Jesus, a friend introduced me to Spiritualism. Spiritualism believes that we can communicate directly with our Loved Ones on the other side—the so called 'dead'. The ministers and students practice their 'intunement', which means the ability to communicate with Spirit. The ministers and some members of the congregation have the gift of Spiritual Mediumship.

Psychics have always intrigued me. A Psychic will tell you what they see about your future, but your future is not really set in stone. We all have the power to choose what action to take. On the other hand, a Medium may pass on messages from loved ones in Spirit, or they may tell you what's going on in your life currently and give you guidance from your Angels. By attending Fraternal Spiritualist Church and taking spiritual development classes with the pastor, Rev. Millie Landis, I began to learn what this kind of communication was all about. Spiritualism also sees Jesus as an Evolved Soul, showing us the way to Love and Service. I began to make a place for Jesus in my life again. It was nice to have Him back.

I learned from Rev. Millie that we all have the ability to communicate, at some level, with Spirit. Some people see images or hear things, while others sense things. I will sometimes hear or see something, but I usually feel the energy. From my gut and body energy I can tell whether something is 'right'—peaceful and life enhancing or 'wrong'—an energy drain and not the best path for me. Spiritualism believes that God, or Spirit, loves us and desires to communicate with us. Since we are Spiritual Beings, we all have the ability to communicate with Spirit. Some of us have developed our ability more than others. Some are born with a very strong, clear, and natural connection to Spirit.

Prior to coming to Spiritualism, I'd had a few experiences where I received messages. I'd see a message flash in front of me, in my mind's eye. This seems to occur when I've been meditating frequently and consistently. The message does not occur while meditating but occurs when I'm going about my day. The first time I experienced this was when I first moved to San Diego. I took a night job at the local hospital, even though it was not a job I particularly wanted. I knew I wanted a position with Student Services at the adult learning school so that I could take classes for free.

One night while on my shift at the hospital, I saw 'CSR' flash in my mind. I thought, "That's right. I need to check the job postings on the web site to see if there are any open positions." I got busy with work and couldn't get to it right away. But later on, when things quieted down, I checked the job board and a position was open! I applied for the position. There were actually three openings. Out of 200 applicants I got one of the positions!

Years later I received another message. I needed to find a dog friendly place to live that was affordable in a location that was safe. I wasn't having any luck. I was about to give up when one morning I saw the word 'Santee' flash across my mind. Santee is a suburb of San Diego. I had looked in that area before but didn't find anything. I decided to follow the guidance I'd received. I got on the computer, looked on Craigslist, where I looked many times before, and there it was: A cottage for rent, within my price range, with a dog friendly landlord. My employer allowed me to switch offices so I could work closer to Santee. I lived there for two very happy years.

Having had these experiences and believing in eternal life, I felt right at home with Spiritualism's teachings. As a former Catholic, I still believed in Angels and welcomed any messages from the Other Side. Rev. Millie has always told us, "When you receive a message from a Spiritual Medium always run it through your God-Self. See if it rings true for you." She also reminds us that we are all Bubbles of God, and, since God is Love, we are Bubbles of Love.

I attended services at Fraternal Spiritualist Church on Sunday and Wednesday evenings. Over a three year period I received many messages. I'll never forget the first message I received from my Dad. It was at a Wednesday night service. Before the service began I told Rev. Millie that it had been five years since my Dad passed away and I hadn't received any messages from him. She said she'd see what she could do about that during the service. I was thrilled when she delivered a message from my Dad. She saw me receiving a trophy for some accomplishment. I recalled when I was in high school receiving a trophy for winning a basketball shooting contest. I took Mom and Dad with me to the award dinner where we had a delicious meal and listened to classical music. Rev. Millie said, "Your Dad feels as proud of you now as he did when you received that trophy." My eyes filled with tears as I soaked up my Dad's love. There's no way Rev. Millie could have known about that experience. It did my heart a world of good to know that, through it all, my Dad was proud of me and was still in my life.

I heard about Rev. Millie's Spiritual Development classes which she held each year. The classes are three hours long. That's right—THREE HOURS LONG. I remember how mortified I was that a class could last THREE HOURS. "What did they do for three hours?" I wondered. It took me awhile before I asked more about the classes, and when I did I heard some pretty amazing testimonials. The healing and spiritual growth that took place in her classes caught my attention. I decided to try it out. What a ride I was in for!

During the first hour of class the group shares God stories. A God Story is when you see the hand of God show-up in your life. Then Rev. Millie shares lessons from her Angel Guides. After a short break, we start the second part of class with a prayer and a song, inviting the Angels and Loved Ones to come in for a visit. This part of class consists of a series of Circles in which messages from Spirit occur. It's important to raise the vibration in the room so that we can reach the Angels and Loved Ones who want to communicate with us. We'll even sing songs during class, mostly Christmas songs and Zippity Do Dah, when prompted by Rev. Millie.

Rev. Millie coaches the class to practice their intunement with Spirit. "Stay alert, everyone," she tells us. She encourages us to trust what we're getting, to share it out loud so everyone can hear us. There are many ways to get a message. People may receive a visual message, like words or pictures. They may also hear something, and sometimes they'll get overcome with emotion. The person receiving the message may know what it means, but if not, Rev. Millie and the other class participants will help sort out the message. For example, if someone is overcome with feelings of regret, it may be another person's Loved One coming in to apologize. The main objective of the class is to know that life is eternal and that your Loved Ones haven't really gone anywhere—they've just left the body—and that they still love you and want to communicate with you.

The first class I attended was amazing. I watched as different Circles developed. One class member was given messages from Spirit which was meant specifically for them. At the beginning of each Circle it is a mystery as to what the message will be. As it develops Rev. Millie gets clearer as to whom (in the class) the Circle is for and what the message is about. The Circle is usually for one of the class participants, but occasionally it's for the entire class. Messages come from the other side to let the person know that their Loved Ones are looking in on them. The class member will receive messages that may provide guidance on their physical journey. The message sometimes conveys love and forgiveness, facilitating healing between the class member and their Loved One who has passed.

Since I was new and the people in class didn't know much about me, Rev. Millie let them practice on me. If the information they received was correct, they proved to me and to themselves that what they were getting was from Spirit. This practice helps to develop and strengthen their spiritual communication. As Rev. Millie often says, "Belief is not enough. You have to **know** that life is eternal."

As the Circle unfolded I received the first message: "You feel guilty about leaving the Catholic Church". My first reaction was "No, I don't. I'm over that" but then I started to cry. I hadn't realized how guilty I still felt over being Gay and leaving the Church. Many Loved Ones came in from the other side: priests and nuns, family and friends. The message was clear: "You needed to leave the Church in order to grow. You wouldn't have grown spiritually if you had stayed. Let go of your guilt. It's weighing you down." I hadn't realized how I still felt like a second class citizen for being Gay. This heavy burden of guilt was draining my energy. Then I heard someone say, "Your Dad is here. He loves you and wants you to be happy." I wanted to be free, to feel lighter, as I continued to live my life. I felt so loved and accepted. My heart was overjoyed.

Many healings took place for my classmates and me. We grew very close as we supported each other through each experience. Rev. Millie gives each class participant their Spirit Guide, which she receives from her Angels. My Spirit Guide is Flying Dove. Flying Dove suggested that, together, we write our God Story in order to assist others on their journey. I've always loved to read and have a fascination with books. I've been known to collect books that I don't make time to read, though I have read quite a few. A couple of years before I received Flying Dove Rev. Millie gave me a message from Spirit: "You have read many books and have studied many things. It's time for you to teach and write your own book." So when I received Flying Dove's message about writing my story I felt it was the right thing to do. It took many rough drafts, many starts and stops, but after three years we've finally completed it!

I had many healing encounters during the three years I took Spiritual Development classes with Rev. Millie. The healing I experienced in more than five years of counseling is nothing to sneeze at. Yet my experiences in her classes were very therapeutic and powerful, so much that I accomplished enormous growth in a short amount of time. My overall vibration has been lightened, allowing more energy to flow through me to live life more fully and effectively. My class experiences also strengthened my self confidence and my spiritual knowing that Love never ends.

One night in class Mary Magdalene came to visit us. Her visit prompted a discussion of who she really was. Mary Magdalene was a Biblical figure, a follower of Jesus, who was thought to be a prostitute. To the contrary, she was not a prostitute, as is commonly believed. There was a mistranslation somewhere along the way. Someone suggested we read the Gnostic Gospel of Thomas to learn more about Mary Magdalene. I ordered a copy so I could learn more about her. I also mentioned this specific class to my dear friend, Jodi. Jodi recommended I read 'The Disappearance of the Universe' as it was about the Gospel of Thomas. She said "If you really get into this book, it will turn your world upside down." I decided I was ready to shake up my life a bit, so I ordered a copy. As I began to read, I couldn't put the book down. It was amazing! The author, Gary Renard, recorded his visits with two Ascendant Masters. These Masters shed light on Jesus' true teachings and how the Bible got many things wrong. It pointed the way to 'A Course in Miracles' (ACIM). Having been intrigued by ACIM for many years, I was excited to gain the knowledge necessary to begin to do the Course.

ACIM is designed to be an individual course of study. It was not intended to become another religion. The power of ACIM is in the Holy Spirit's ability to change the reader's perceptions. The Course is actually taught by Jesus and the Holy Spirit. How nice to cut out the 'middle man'! I'm very grateful to Gary Renard for being willing to share his story in 'The Disappearance of the Universe' so that more people can truly understand ACIM and apply it in their own lives. I encourage you to read 'The Disappearance of the Universe', especially if you've been struggling to understand the Course. The Course has simplified my life by putting things in perspective.

My desire for further growth led me to the teachings of Science of Mind. Louise L. Hay started her career as a Spiritual Practitioner through Science of Mind (SOM). She used SOM principles in her sessions along with Spiritual Mind Treatments and affirmations. It's funny how 'coincidence' leads you where you need to be. One of my previous sponsors used to say, "Coincidence is God's way of remaining anonymous." She called it 'God-incidence'.

After attending the Spiritualist Church for a couple of years I was introduced to OM Center for Spiritual Living, a new Science of Mind Center which was started by Rev. Suzette Wehunt. Occasionally I attended services on Sunday morning. Then I wanted to learn more about its teachings, so I began taking classes. Along the way I decided to become a Spiritual Practitioner. Being a Practitioner is a great way to combine my love for coaching and my passion for ministering to other's spiritual needs. Becoming a Spiritual Practitioner seems like an ultimate God-calling for me.

The name Science of Mind comes from the idea that God is in everything and therefore, God is All there is. And All is in the Mind of God. Science comes from how Mind works scientifically, which means, like science, Mind is consistent and results can be duplicated. God, or Mind, is creative, and as we plant our thoughts into God's creative energy, we will manifest what we've intended, if it is for our highest good.

By attending OM I was being fed intellectually, yet it wasn't all 'heady'. I felt peaceful and positive as I claimed my Oneness with God and others. Science of Mind teaches much of what I already believe. It emphasizes meditation and the power of our thoughts. Our thoughts and beliefs create our own experience. Does this sound familiar?

At OM Center, I was introduced to a powerful healing technique called Spiritual Mind Treatment. The classes increased my comfort level in doing Treatment (also called Affirmative Prayer) for myself and others. Here's a brief prayer example:

I know that God is all there is and I am one with God.
I know and accept that perfect health is mine right now.
I give thanks for this truth, knowing that it is so.
I release it to the Law of Mind—and So It Is.

You claim it, affirm it, feel it, give thanks and release it to God's Loving Power. Confidence in your prayer is very important. If doubt enters later on, do another treatment and do it consistently until you can feel it, believe it, and know it—just like with any affirmation.

I love the teachings of Ernest Holmes, the founder of Science of Mind. I also love Spiritualism. My desire is to unite the two. For me, these two approaches complement each other very well. SOM teaches how to approach daily living effectively while Spiritualism reminds us of our eternal connection with God and Spirit so we need never feel alone.

 **Reflection**

My journey has taken me full circle. I started with God's Love and I continue with God's Love—in my heart and in my life. The purpose of this journey is to help you become more aware of who you really are—Love. What can you do today to express your Loving Self?

Closing Thoughts

Though my journey has taken me to different places I am grateful for the gifts Catholicism gave me: my love for Jesus, Mary, the Saints and my awareness of Angels. Catholicism led me to the Convent where I got sober and began to live a more spiritual life.

I was required to read several books before entering the Convent, one of which was 'Hinds Feet on High Places.' I identified with the main character, Much Afraid. Much Afraid trusted the Shepherd to take her to the High Places, but first she had to find the courage and strength to leave her family and her fears behind. At the end of the journey she earned a new name: Accept with Joy. The Bible says, "Perfect Love casts out all fear." By letting go of my fears, working through my issues and allowing Love in, I've become much lighter and experience acceptance and joy in my life.

I hope that you found my story uplifting and inspiring. Thank you for taking this journey with me. Reflect on your own journey and follow wherever Spirit is leading you. We are all One in Spirit and need each other to bring more Light and Love into the world. I truly appreciate the part you play and bless you on your way.

Appendix A

The Story Behind the Music

Before I came out in 1988, Grandma passed away from cancer. I was home when she was diagnosed and was able to see her one last time while she was in the hospital. She remained strong, saying "What are you going to do?" There was about a month between her diagnosis and her passing. During that time I was back in St. Louis, starting another semester of college. My grief was heavy and distracting. I cried and prayed and longed to be close to my Grandma once again. One night I went to my favorite golf course, near an Al-Anon meeting I attended regularly, and wrote this song for Grandma. I was able to share it at her memorial service.

For Grandma

You'll always be a part of my life—yes you will
Though it hurts to know that I must let you go
You'll always be a part of my life

You have a special place in my heart—yes you do
With your smiling eyes—and your warm goodbyes
You have a special place in my heart

The love you gave to us was so true
There'll never be a more wonderful Grandma than you
Your chocolate chip cookies are known throughout the land
Just one of the many gifts of love from your hand

Though it's sad to see an era of my life pass away
And I begged to God to please let you stay
Sauerbraten and dumplings remind me of the many things
That you gave to us in your special way

Before this song comes to a close I must add one last thing
You're here inside my heart whenever I sing
Your beautiful voice singing love songs everywhere
Fill my memories with joy beyond compare
You'll always be a part of my life . . .

'Children of the Light' was inspired by a few things. First, I read an article in a metaphysical magazine shortly after Coming Out which referred to us as Children of Light. At that time I was struggling with rejection by my former sponsor due to being Gay. She was a Christian and her judgment was very hurtful. I knew that, as a child of God, I was Ok with God and that I was loved unconditionally.

Children of the Light

You have a plan for me
To be all I can be
And all I want to do
Is share my love for You
So take me by the hand
Help me to understand
How to share Your Love with all Your children

You see, it doesn't matter where we come from
It doesn't matter where we've been
It doesn't matter if we're male or female
Nor the color of our skin
It doesn't matter who we love
For all love comes from God above
All that matters is to know that we belong

Yes, We are Children of the Light
Lighting up the World
Making it Bright with the Light of God's Love
Yes, We are Children of the Light
Lighting up the World
Making it Bright with the Light of God's Love

One day I was cleaning house for a family with little children. Looking around at the toys in the little boy's bedroom, I began to wonder how children see God. "If I had a child in front of me who didn't know anything about God, what would I want to tell them?" I thought. I wrote this song to the tune of 'We Love You Conrad' from the play 'Bye, Bye, Birdie.'

There Is a Power

There is a Power
Oh way up high
Who made the moon, the stars, and the sky
And when I feel the Sun's warm glow
I know this Power loves me so

There is a Power
Both far and wide
Who made the ocean shore
And mountain side
The roaring of the waves and gentle breeze
Stirs this Power inside of me

There is a Power
Both far and near
No matter where I am
Is present here
To love and guide me with tender care
Yes, my Power is always there
Thank-God my Power is always there

105

One summer I worked at a summer camp. We made a field trip to Amaghetti's Bakery, in St. Louis, and had a meeting with the founder, Mrs. Amaghetti. She shared her philosophy: "Believe in yourself, Trust in God and Follow Your Dreams." She inspired me to write this song:

Follow Your Dreams

Believe in Yourself, Trust in God, Follow Your Dreams
For as simple as these three may seem
They are vital to life—help in overcoming strife
Believe in Yourself, Trust in God, Follow Your Dreams

When I was young I dreamed many dreams
Saw many visions of how life could be
Now one of my dreams has come true
For here I am singing to you

Now if you are down, alone and feeling blue
Wondering why your dreams have not come true
Take it from one who knows
Action makes your dreams go, so . . . .
Believe in Yourself, Trust in God, Follow Your Dreams

Sue and I also got involved with Alateen and Trend, two teen organizations in St. Louis. Initially we were told that the teens wouldn't like our folk music. They were into Rap. I felt hurt and rejected. So one day while cleaning house, I started to rap out this song:

I'm Worth It

When times are tough and you want to run
Life it seems just ain't much fun
You're feeling such intense pain
You wonder if you'll ever be happy again
Then a so-called friend walks up to you
Says try some of this—it'll get you through

You look them in the eye and you say "No Way—
I'm not gonna be your fool today"
Then you think to yourself
Now I know what to do—
I've gotta find a true friend I can talk to
Someone I trust who will understand
Someone to lend me a helping hand
Cuz I'm Worth It
More than money can buy
I'm Worth It
I need a natural high
I'm Worth It
Make My dreams come true
I'm Worth It—(I'm gonna follow through)
And so are You!

I took a semester of music while thinking about becoming a music therapist. During my guitar class I had to write a blues song. I had a history with Yukon Jack as well as Jack Daniels. My friend Barb helped me flush it out from my original three verses to six:

YUKON JACK DANIELS
Blues Song

Verse One
Yukon Jack Daniels—thought they were friends of mine
I said, Yukon Jack Daniels—thought they were friends of mine
In their company—I'd feel so fine.

Verse Two
Now, Yukon Jack Daniels—brought only misery
I said, Yukon Jack Daniels—brought only misery
One day I realized—they had a hold on me.

Verse Three
So I said, "Yukon Jack Daniels—now are you friend or foe?"
I said, "Yukon Jack Daniels—are you friend or foe?
If you cause me pain—I've gotta let you go."

Verse Four

Now Yukon Jack Daniels—You got me wailing the blues
I said, Yukon Jack Daniels—You got me wailing the blues
I woke up one morning—knew I had to choose.

Verse Five

Yukon Jack Daniels—You're just no good for me
I said, Yukon Jack Daniels—You're just no good for me
Now I'm sober, happy, joyous and free.

Verse Six

Now the only time I sing the blues—is when I give up on me
I said, the only time I sing the blues—is when I give up on me
Now I have the tools—to be all I can be.

As you can see, my songs were inspired by a variety of circumstances. One particular influence came from the Missouri School for the Blind, where Sue had gone to school years earlier. I lived close to the school and drove by quite often. They had inspirational quotes on a sign in their yard. A few of my songs were inspired by those quotes. For example, one day the sign said: "If your ship doesn't come in, then swim out to it," which is a quote attributed to Jonathan Winters. This quote resonated with me about sharing my music. I thought, "No matter what happens, I will continue to sing!" The second verse came from a joke that Father Joseph Martin often told about God telling us to 'let go and trust'. Here's the song:

Just Do It

If your ship don't come in—then swim out to it
No sense waiting around
Come On, Just Do It
You know you can—You've Got that Power Within
So Use It—Or Lose It

It's like walking on water—making a leap of faith
When you'd rather stay at home where it's nice and safe
But that Voice inside won't leave you in peace

Til you follow where it leads—No matter where it be, yeah!

It's like hanging from a limb—trying hard to hold on
Your fingers growing numb—all your strength is gone
Then a Voice above says "Will you trust me now?
If you will just let go—I will show you how." Yeah!

Another quote said something like, "When you're climbing a ladder, don't just stand there. Use the rungs of the ladder to move up to where you want to be." I saw the rungs as the 12 Steps and other tools I'd learned and used in my recovery.

Move It On Up

When you hit a brick wall and there's no way around it
Don't bang your head
Grab a ladder instead

Use the rung of the ladder to move on up
Rest if you must but don't give up
Your strength will return and you will learn
You've got the power to move it on up, on up
You've got the power to move it on up

Don't let an obstacle get you down
A little perseverance will turn it around
Rely on the ladder and you will find
Pleasant surprises on the other side

Sometimes I read a book that inspired me to write a song. Marianne Williamson's book *Illuminata* inspired the song below. You can imagine the thrill it gave Sue and I when we shared this song in prison and the inmates joined us on the chorus.

Teach Only Love

Teach only Love—Teach only Peace
Surrender all your hate—and let the violence cease

Reach out your hand—place it in mine
And let's create a Peace to last for all time

We are unique—We are the same
I need you and you need me
There's no room for blame
I see your fear—I've been there too
But walking side by side
There's nothing we can't do

I read a book from M. Scott Peck called 'What Return Can I Make', which inspired this song:

Make Me New

When I am broken I come to You
For in my brokenness I'm made whole and new
Your Love heals me through and through
You long for me – I long to be with You
My brokenness has made me New

In my naiveté I said 'Yes, Lord'
Not knowing where the path would lead
But once again I fall and crawl back to You
I surrender, Lord, it's You I need

Lord, You give us Power—to create Love on Earth
In accepting our limitations
We know what Your Love is Worth

'Dream Again' was written when I was listening to the Indigo Girls music. I love their harmony and their song writing and musical abilities. I was feeling inadequate and writing this song renewed my passion and commitment to sharing my music.

Dream Again

I've got a dream to follow—"Don't waste your time"
I've got a song to sing—"It's not as good as mine"
I've got love to share—"Well, ask me if I care"
Well I do

I'm keeping the Faith everyday
No doubt or fear will get in my way
My Higher Power has a plan
And with This Power I know that I can
I'll keep the faith—give it another try
My only limit is the sky
I've got nothing to lose—everything to gain
So I'll open my heart
And Dream Again
Oh, Dream Again

I've got a dream to follow—"Go for It"
I've got a song to sing—"Let us hear it"
I've got love to share—Come share it with me

Oh, I'm keeping the Faith everyday
No doubt or fear will get in my way
My Higher Power has a plan
And with This Power I know that I can
I'll keep the faith—give it another try
My only limit is the sky
I've got nothing to lose—everything to gain
So I'll open my heart
And Dream Again
Oh, Dream Again

Appendix B

Recommended Reading List

1. The Power of Positive Thinking—Norman Vincent Peale

2. Hinds Feet on High Places—Hanna Hurnard

3. Adult Children of Alcoholics—Janet Woititz

4. Codependent No More—Melody Beattie

5. Beyond Codependency—Melody Beattie

6. The Language of Letting Go—Melody Beattie

7. Daily Affirmations for Adult Children—Rochelle Lerner

8. The Little Prince—Antoine De Saint—Exupery

9. Embraced By the Light—Betty J. Eadie

10. The Road Less Traveled—M. Scott Peck

11. A Return to Love—Marianne Williamson

12. Illuminata—Marianne Williamson

13. The Seven Spiritual Laws of Success—Deepak Chopra

14. You Can Heal Your Life—Louise L. Hay

15. I Can Do It—Louise L. Hay

16. Ordering from the Cosmic Kitchen—Dr. Patricia Crane

17. Zero Limits—Joe Vitale and Ihaleakala Hew Len, PhD

18. Ask and It Is Given—Esther and Jerry Hicks and anything from Abraham—Hicks (The Teachings of Abraham)

19. The Power of Intention—Dr. Wayne W. Dyer

20. Change Your Thoughts—Change Your Life—Living the Wisdom of the Tao—Dr. Wayne W. Dyer

21. Unlimit Your Life: Getting and Setting Goals—Dr. James Fadiman

22. The Big Picture – The Seven Step Guide For Creative Success in Business – The Business Book for Artists by RD Riccoboni

23. The Science of Mind: The Complete Edition—Ernest Holmes

24. The Essential Ernest Holmes

25. The Sermon on the Mount – Emmet Fox

26. To Touch an Angel – Rev. Millie Landis

27. Full Disclosure – Lives and Lessons in Spiritualism By Cheryl L. Lehman and Rev. Mildred Landis

28. The Disappearance of the Universe—Gary R. Renard

29. Your Immortal Reality—Gary R. Renard

30. A Course In Miracles—Foundation For Inner Peace

About the Author

Kathy Stolecki is a singer/songwriter, life coach and motivational speaker. Her speaking style is unique as she incorporates her music into her presentations. She loves to share about Spiritualism, Science of Mind and A Course in Miracles. She works with those recovering from addiction and those who want to empower themselves and create the life of their dreams. Kathy is trained in addiction recovery, grief and loss support and Science of Mind principles. With over 25 years of recovery from alcoholism and codependency, Kathy ministers from a place of empathy and compassion. She loves to empower others to find and live their life's purpose. She lives with her partner in California. For more information, visit her website:

www.KathyStolecki.com or www.WakingUpSober.com

Be The Light You Were Born To Be
Let the Love Within You Set You Free
For God is Love and So are We
Shine Your Light for All to See

Pass it on - Live Joyously!!!

Made in United States
Orlando, FL
24 February 2022

15122480R00075